AP U.S. HISTORY FLASHCARDS

Premium Edition with CD-ROM

Test-Readiness Quizzes
with Instant Scoring

PLUS U.S. History
Timelines

Kwynn Olson
AP U.S. History Teacher
Bolingbrook High School
Bolingbrook, Illinois

Mark Bach
AP History Teacher
Seattle, Washington

Research & Education Association
Visit our website at: www.rea.com

Research & Education Association
61 Ethel Road West
Piscataway, New Jersey 08854
E-mail: info@rea.com

REA's Flashcard Book for the AP U.S. History Exam Premium Edition with CD-ROM

Published 2011

Printed in the United States of America

Library of Congress Control Number 2008941410

ISBN 13: 978-0-7386-0503-6
ISBN 10: 0-7386-0503-4

About This Premium Edition with CD-ROM

REA's unique Premium Edition Flashcard Book features questions and answers to help you study for the Advanced Placement United States History Exam. This book, enhanced with an interactive CD-ROM, is designed to fit conveniently into your study schedule for AP United States History. You'll find it's an especially effective study tool when paired with *REA's AP United States History,* our celebrated comprehensive review and practice-exam book.

This handy volume is filled with 1,000 must-study AP United States History questions and detailed answers. The questions are chronologically ordered and cover all topics found on the AP United States History exam from Pre-Columbian societies to the present. The full index makes it easy to look up a particular subject and review a specific historical time period.

Unlike most flashcards that come loose in a box, these flashcards are bound in an easy-to-use, organized book. This innovative Flashcard Book lets you write your answer to a question on the front of the card, and then compare it to the answer on the back of the card. REA's flashcards are a great way to boost your test-readiness and are perfect for studying on the go.

The interactive CD-ROM includes four test-readiness quizzes, timelines of all chronological periods covered on the actual AP exam, and a concise United States History review.

This Premium Edition Flashcard Book has been carefully developed with REA's customary concern for excellence. We believe you will find it an outstanding addition to your AP United States History prep.

Larry B. Kling
Chief Editor

About the Authors

Kwynn Olson is an AP United States History teacher at Bolingbrook High School in Bolingbrook, Illinois. Mr. Olson received his B.S. in Social Studies Secondary Education and his M.A. in Leadership in Education Administration from Bradley University.

Mark Bach, author of our CD-ROM quizzes, has been teaching AP History courses since 1983 and is currently an on-line instructor at APEX Learning in Seattle, Washington. Mr. Bach received his B.A. in History, German and Religion from St. Olaf College in Minnesota and his M.A. from Michigan State University.

About Research & Education Association

Founded in 1959, Research & Education Association (REA) is dedicated to publishing the finest and most effective educational materials—including software, study guides, and test preps—for students in middle school, high school, college, graduate school, and beyond.

We invite you to visit us at *www.rea.com* to find out how "REA is making the world smarter."

Acknowledgments

In addition to our author, we would like to thank Larry B. Kling, Vice President, Editorial, for his overall guidance, which brought this publication to completion; Pam Weston, Vice President, Publishing, for setting the quality standards for production integrity and managing the publication to completion; John Cording, Vice President, Technology, for coordinating the design and development of REA's CD software; Diane Goldschmidt, Senior Editor, for editorial project management; Alice Leonard, Senior Editor, for preflight editorial review; Heena Patel and Amy Jamison, Technology Project Managers, for their design contributions and software testing efforts; Jeff LoBalbo, Senior Graphic Designer, for coordinating pre-press electronic file mapping; and Christine Saul, Senior Graphic Designer, for designing our cover.

We also extend special thanks to Caroline Duffy and Marianne L'Abbate for copyediting, Hadassa Goldsmith for proofreading, and Kathy Caratozzolo of Caragraphics for typesetting this edition.

Table of Contents

Test-Readiness Quizzes on CD

After studying questions 1 through 237, take Quiz 1.
Take Quiz 2 after studying questions 238 through 489.
After studying questions 490 through 696, take Quiz 3.
Quiz 4 starts after question 1000.

Questions

Q–1

Why did the Spaniards begin importing African slaves?

Your Answer _____

_____

Q–2

Who were the *peninsulares*?

Your Answer _____

_____

Q–3

_____ were individuals of Spanish parentage who had been born in the New World.

Your Answer _____

_____

Correct Answers

A–1

African slaves were imported to meet the Spaniards' labor needs, especially as the Indian population had been decimated by disease and overwork.

A–2

The *peninsulares* were natives of Spain who were ranked at the top of New Spain's rigidly stratified society.

A–3

Creoles

Questions

Q–4

Why did the English colonists enjoy a greater degree of freedom from government interference?

Your Answer _____

_____

Q–5

What is the oldest city in North America?

Your Answer _____

_____

Q–6

What colony was founded by Sir Walter Raleigh? What happened to this colony?

Your Answer _____

_____

Correct Answers

A–4

English colonizing efforts were supported by private, rather than government, funds.

A–5

St. Augustine, Florida

A–6

1) Roanoke Island
2) The colony was deserted. No one knows what happened to the colonists.

Questions

Q–7

List three reasons why English interest in American colonization subsided after the Roanoke experiment failed.

Your Answer _____

_____

Q–8

What was Great Britain's first permanent settlement in the New World? What happened at this colony?

Your Answer _____

_____

Q–9

How was Jamestown saved?

Your Answer _____

_____

Correct Answers

A–7

1) England was hampered by an ongoing war with Spain.
2) It had inadequate financial resources.
3) It had unrealistic expectations for successfully colonizing the New World.

A–8

1) Jamestown, Virginia
2) The colony suffered from disease due to the swampy environment where it was settled. Also, during the "starving time," many colonists died because many settlers were looking for wealth and not planting sufficient crops. The colony also suffered attacks from hostile Indians.

A–9

When John Smith arrived, he required all those who wished to eat, to work. Later on, John Rolfe introduced better farming techniques for growing tobacco, which became the backbone of the Virginian economy.

Questions

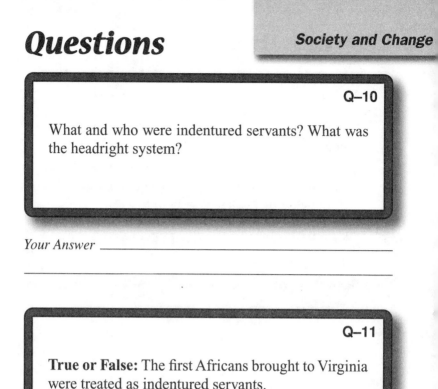

Q–10

What and who were indentured servants? What was the headright system?

Your Answer _____

_____

Q–11

True or False: The first Africans brought to Virginia were treated as indentured servants.

Your Answer _____

_____

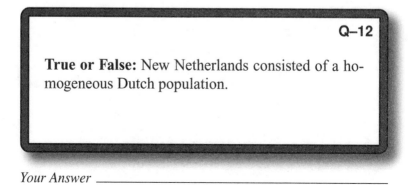

Q–12

True or False: New Netherlands consisted of a homogeneous Dutch population.

Your Answer _____

_____

Correct Answers

A–10

1) Indentured servants were people who exchanged their labor for passage to the New World. Many times, these were sons who, due to primogeniture and the excessive labor supply in England, had few economic prospects at home.
2) The headright system gave grants of lands in the New World to those who paid the passage of indentured servants.

A–11

True

A–12

False. The New Netherlands consisted of a mixture of people from all over Europe and many African slaves.

Questions

Q–13

The two religious groups that settled Plymouth Colony were _____ and _____.

Your Answer _____

Q–14

Under whose leadership was the Massachusetts Bay Colony founded?

Your Answer _____

Q–15

_____ _____, a dissident Puritan minister, founded the settlement of Providence.

Your Answer _____

Correct Answers

A–13

Puritans and Separatists

A–14

John Winthrop

A–15

Roger Williams

Q–16

True or False: Anne Hutchinson was banished from the Massachusetts Bay Colony for being a witch.

Your Answer _____

_____

Q–17

True or False: In the 1630s, England stopped granting charters to joint-stock companies and began granting them to individuals or groups of individuals.

Your Answer _____

_____

Q–18

What was the first proprietary colony?

Your Answer _____

_____

Correct Answers

A–16

False. Anne Hutchinson was banished for openly challenging religious Puritan doctrine.

A–17

True

A–18

Maryland

Questions

Q–19

Which colony served as a refuge for English Catholics?

Your Answer _____

Q–20

Why was the Act of Religious Toleration approved in Maryland?

Your Answer _____

Q–21

Which colony was largely settled by an English planter class from Barbados?

Your Answer _____

Correct Answers

Maryland

The Act of Religious Toleration was intended to protect the Catholic minority by granting freedom of worship to all Christian persuasions.

South Carolina

Q–22

True or False: Charles II granted eight English noblemen a charter for the lands lying south of Virginia and north of Spanish Florida for helping him regain his throne.

Your Answer _____

_____

Q–23

Why did the Carolinas attract few settlers?

Your Answer _____

_____

Q–24

Apart from an increase in immigration, list two reasons for an increase in New England's population.

Your Answer _____

_____

Correct Answers

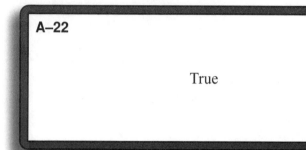

A–22

True

A–23

The proprietors set up a hierarchal, almost feudal, society that proved to be totally unworkable.

A–24

1) Typical New England families had more children than did their British counterparts.
2) More New England children survived to adulthood than did their English contemporaries.

Q–25

True or False: In the seventeenth century, a New Englander could expect to live ten to fifteen years longer than his English contemporary.

Your Answer _____

_____

Q–26

Why did the New England colonists enjoy a more stable and well-ordered society than the Chesapeake Bay colonists?

Your Answer _____

_____

Q–27

True or False: By the 1750s, black slaves made up 30 to 40 percent of the Chesapeake Bay colonies' population.

Your Answer _____

_____

Correct Answers

A–25

False. A New Englander could expect to live twenty-five to thirty years longer than an Englishman.

A–26

Unlike the Chesapeake Bay colonists, New Englanders had migrated as family units and had a more homogeneous population.

A–27

True

Questions

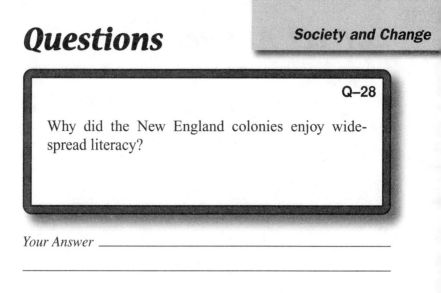

Q–28

Why did the New England colonies enjoy wide-spread literacy?

Your Answer _____

_____

Q–29

Which Massachusetts city became an international port?

Your Answer _____

_____

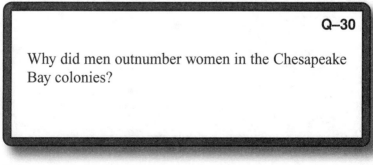

Q–30

Why did men outnumber women in the Chesapeake Bay colonies?

Your Answer _____

_____

Correct Answers

A–28

Puritans placed a great emphasis on reading because they believed that everyone should be able to read the Bible.

A–29

Boston

A–30

Most Chesapeake settlers came to the colonies as indentured servants to work in the tobacco fields.

Q–31

What was Bacon's Rebellion and what was its effect?

Your Answer _____

_____

Q–32

What was the Half-way Covenant and what was its purpose?

Your Answer _____

_____

Q–33

True or False: The Puritans were unsuccessful in converting the majority of Indians to Christianity.

Your Answer _____

_____

Correct Answers

A–31

1) Nathaniel Bacon led a group of men, many of them former indentured servants, in burning Jamestown to show their disapproval of the colony's Indian policy.
2) It marked the turning point from the use of indentured servants to the use of African slave labor.

A–32

1) The Half-way Covenant was a policy in the Puritan church that provided partial church membership for the children of members who did not profess saving grace.
2) It was intended to keep the membership rolls full and maintain the church's influence in society. Many Puritan ministers denounced it in sermons known as jeremiads.

A–33

True. Most Indians remained unconverted.

Questions

Q–34

What are some of the explanations as to why the Salem witch trials occurred?

Your Answer _____

_____

Q–35

In contrast to the Puritans, _____ believed that all persons had an "inner light," which allowed them to communicate with God.

Your Answer _____

_____

Q–36

Who founded Pennsylvania? Why was Pennsylvania founded?

Your Answer _____

_____

Correct Answers

A–34

1) Religious differences between the members and nonmembers of the Congregational Church
2) Socioeconomic differences between the poorer farmers in the west and the wealthier merchants in the east

A–35

Quakers

A–36

1) William Penn
2) He founded Pennsylvania as a haven for Quakers, a religious sect whose followers were pacifists and believed all people had an "inner light" that allowed them to communicate with God.

Q–37

List three incentives offered by William Penn to attract people to his colony.

Your Answer _____

_____

Q–38

Apart from the English, which other groups immigrated to America during the early 1700s?

Your Answer _____

_____

Q–39

List three reasons why the Germans immigrated to America in the early 1700s.

Your Answer _____

_____

Correct Answers

A–37

Full religious freedom, generous terms on land, and a representative assembly

A–38

Scots-Irish and Germans

A–39

Wars, poverty, and religious persecution in their homeland

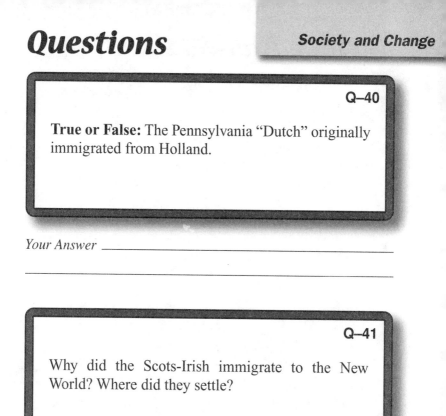

Q–40

True or False: The Pennsylvania "Dutch" originally immigrated from Holland.

Your Answer _____

_____

Q–41

Why did the Scots-Irish immigrate to the New World? Where did they settle?

Your Answer _____

_____

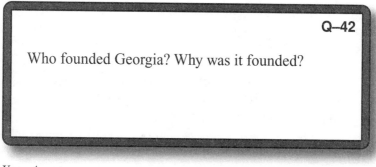

Q–42

Who founded Georgia? Why was it founded?

Your Answer _____

_____

Correct Answers

A–40

False. They were from Germany.

A–41

1) The Scots-Irish left their homelands due to high rent and economic depression.
2) They settled in the Virginia and North Carolina mountain valleys, beyond the Appalachians.

A–42

1) General James Oglethorpe
2) He founded Georgia to be a buffer zone between the English settlements in North America and Spanish-controlled Florida.

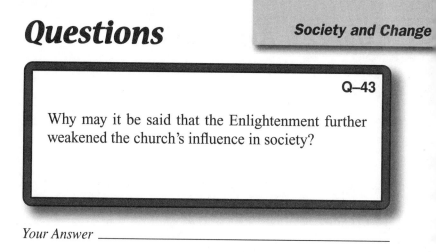

Q–43

Why may it be said that the Enlightenment further weakened the church's influence in society?

Your Answer _____

_____

Q–44

What was the Great Awakening?

Your Answer _____

_____

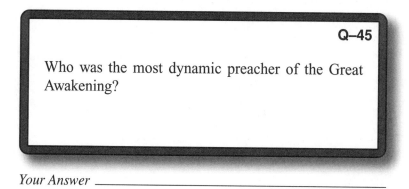

Q–45

Who was the most dynamic preacher of the Great Awakening?

Your Answer _____

_____

Correct Answers

A–43

The Enlightenment placed less faith in God as an active force in the universe.

A–44

The Great Awakening was a series of religious revivals throughout the colonies between 1720 and 1740.

A–45

George Whitefield

Questions

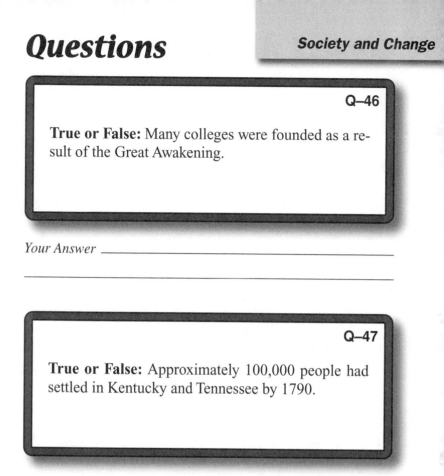

Q-46

True or False: Many colleges were founded as a result of the Great Awakening.

Your Answer _____

Q-47

True or False: Approximately 100,000 people had settled in Kentucky and Tennessee by 1790.

Your Answer _____

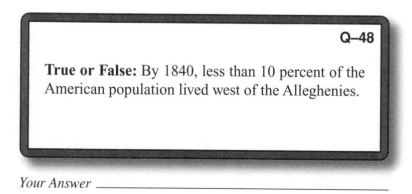

Q-48

True or False: By 1840, less than 10 percent of the American population lived west of the Alleghenies.

Your Answer _____

Correct Answers

True. These colleges were established primarily for the purpose of training New Light ministers.

True

False. Over one-third of the population lived there.

Questions

Q–49

Instead of being prepared for academic training, women were generally taught _____ skills.

Your Answer _____

_____

Q–50

What was the Second Great Awakening?

Your Answer _____

_____

Q–51

Why did the birthrate begin to drop, especially in the cities, after 1800?

Your Answer _____

_____

Correct Answers

A–49

homemaking

A–50

The Second Great Awakening was a revival that took place in the beginning of the 1800s. Women and blacks were heavily involved in the movement, and it sparked the reforms of the 1830s and 1840s.

A–51

Children were becoming liabilities rather than assets.

Q–52

During the early part of the nineteenth century, the only professional training was in the subject of _____.

Your Answer _____

_____

Q–53

In the early decades of the nineteenth century, the population of Virginia and the Carolinas shifted to which three states in the lower South?

Your Answer _____

_____

Q–54

As the nineteenth century progressed, which section of the country did the expanding West come to identify with?

Your Answer _____

_____

Correct Answers

A–52

theology

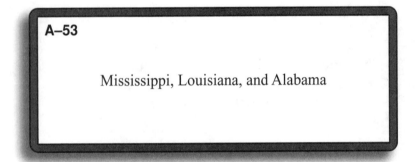

A–53

Mississippi, Louisiana, and Alabama

A–54

The North

Questions

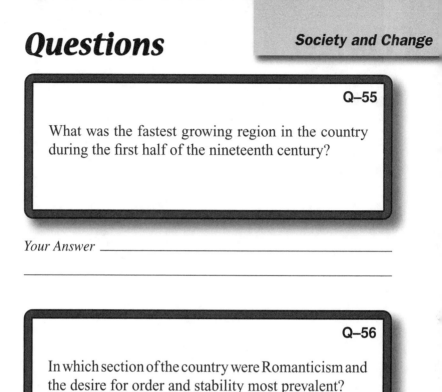

Q–55

What was the fastest growing region in the country during the first half of the nineteenth century?

Your Answer _____

_____

Q–56

In which section of the country were Romanticism and the desire for order and stability most prevalent?

Your Answer _____

_____

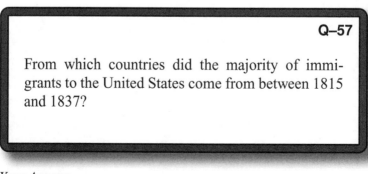

Q–57

From which countries did the majority of immigrants to the United States come from between 1815 and 1837?

Your Answer _____

_____

Correct Answers

A–55

The West

A–56

In the Northeast, especially New England

A–57

Britain, Germany, and southern Ireland

Questions

Q–58

What immigrant group was the target of job discrimination during the first half of the nineteenth century?

Your Answer _____

Q–59

True or False: After 1830, a strong anti-Catholic element was strengthened after waves of immigrants came to America from Catholic Ireland and southern Germany.

Your Answer _____

Q–60

Who supported and opposed the temperance movement in the nineteenth century?

Your Answer _____

Correct Answers

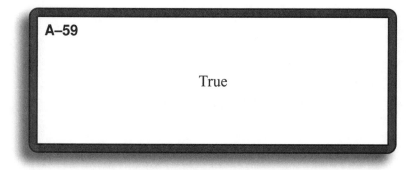

A–58

Irish Catholics

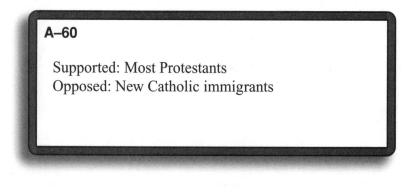

A–59

True

A–60

Supported: Most Protestants
Opposed: New Catholic immigrants

Questions

Q–61

Which section of the country had the fewest number of public schools in the 1830s?

Your Answer _____

_____

Q–62

What colony was established for freed slaves in 1830?

Your Answer _____

_____

Q–63

List several problems that persisted in urban areas during the 1830s and 1840s.

Your Answer _____

_____

Correct Answers

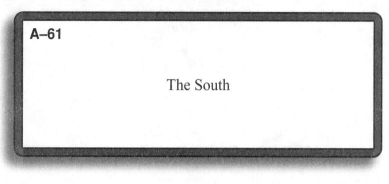

A–61

The South

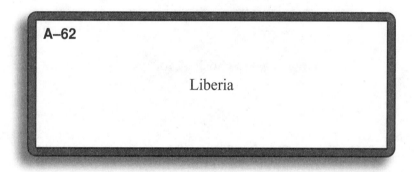

A–62

Liberia

A–63

Bad water, poor sanitation, poor housing and transportation, and inadequate fire and police protection

Questions

Q–64

Who was Sam Houston?

Your Answer _____

_____

Q–65

What encouraged 6,000 Americans to travel westward over the Oregon Trail during the first half of the 1840s?

Your Answer _____

_____

Q–66

Who founded the Church of Jesus Christ of Latter Day Saints? Where did followers of this religion finally settle in 1846? What controversial practice was banned before statehood would be granted?

Your Answer _____

_____

Correct Answers

A–64

Sam Houston won Texas's independence from Mexico on April 23, 1836.

A–65

Reports by fur traders and missionaries about Oregon's favorable soil and climate

A–66

1) Joseph Smith
2) Brigham Young helped the Mormons settle around the Great Salt Lake in what would become the Utah Territory.
3) Polygamy

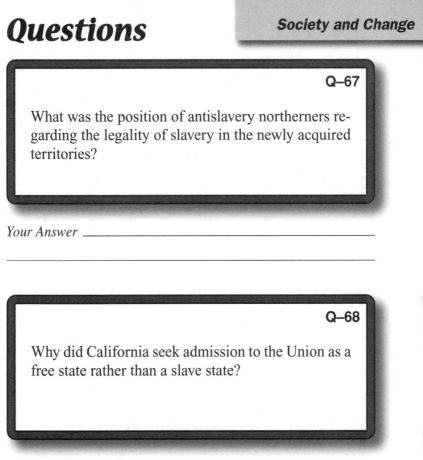

Q–67

What was the position of antislavery northerners regarding the legality of slavery in the newly acquired territories?

Your Answer _____

_____

Q–68

Why did California seek admission to the Union as a free state rather than a slave state?

Your Answer _____

_____

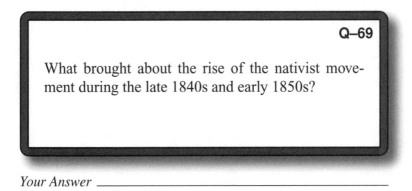

Q–69

What brought about the rise of the nativist movement during the late 1840s and early 1850s?

Your Answer _____

_____

Correct Answers

A–67

Antislavery northerners felt that Congress had the right to prohibit slavery in the territories, based on the Northwest Ordinance of 1787 and the Missouri Compromise of 1820.

A–68

Few slaveholders had come to California because its lawless atmosphere threatened their investment in slaves.

A–69

The alarm of native-born Americans over the rising tide of German and Irish immigration

Q–70

What was the New England Emigrant Aid Company?

Your Answer _____

_____

Q–71

Who constantly threatened the economic security of free blacks living in the cities during the 1850s?

Your Answer _____

_____

Q–72

Where did most of the people who settled in Kansas during the 1850s come from? What was their attitude toward slavery?

Your Answer _____

_____

Correct Answers

A–70

An organization formed by northerners to promote the settling of antislavery men in Kansas

A–71

Newly arrived immigrants who were willing to work for the least desirable jobs for lower wages

A–72

1) They were midwesterners in search of good farmland.
2) They were generally opposed to the spread of slavery.

Questions

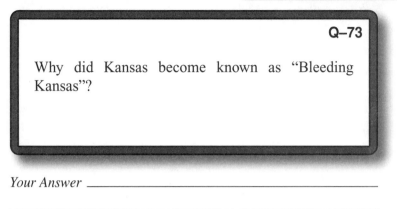

Q–73

Why did Kansas become known as "Bleeding Kansas"?

Your Answer _____

_____

Q–74

What were the Sack of Lawrence and the Pottawatomie Massacre?

Your Answer _____

_____

Q–75

Why did Congressman Preston Brooks beat Senator Charles Sumner unconscious with a cane?

Your Answer _____

_____

Correct Answers

A–73

Full-scale guerilla war erupted there after the election of two opposing territorial governments.

A–74

Both occurred during the guerrilla war in "Bleeding Kansas." At the Sack of Lawrence, pro-slavery forces attacked free-soilers. In response, John Brown led antislavery forces in slaughtering several pro-slavery supporters at the Pottawatomie Massacre.

A–75

Senator Sumner had delivered a two-day antislavery speech titled "The Crime Against Kansas" that insulted Congressman Brooks's uncle and South Carolina. This represented a more violent turn in the slavery controversy.

Questions

Q–76

What was the purpose of John Brown's raid on Harper's Ferry? What was the reaction to this event?

Your Answer _____

_____

Q–77

True or False: By 1860, the population in the West had tripled since 1790.

Your Answer _____

_____

Q–78

By 1860, _____ percent of the U.S. population lived in cities.

Your Answer _____

_____

Correct Answers

A–76

1) John Brown hoped to capture the federal arsenal and start a slave uprising.
2) Many in the North began to view Brown as a martyr, but many in the South saw this as evidence that the North wanted to end slavery. This event also played on one of the South's deepest fears, slave revolt.

A–77

False. The population was eight times that of the 1790 population, growing from 4 million to 32 million people.

A–78

25

Questions

Q–79

True or False: Between 1800 and 1860, the purchasing power of the average worker remained the same.

Your Answer _____

Q–80

True or False: The majority of southerners owned slaves.

Your Answer _____

Q–81

Which class had economic power and dominated the political and social life of the South?

Your Answer _____

Correct Answers

A–79

False. It doubled.

A–80

False. Three-fourths of the southern whites did not own any slaves.

A–81

The planter class

Q–82

How did the gang system operate on large southern plantations?

Your Answer _____

_____

Q–83

What were the benefits and drawbacks of being a house slave instead of a field hand?

Your Answer _____

_____

Q–84

True or False: A sizeable number of black slaves worked in towns serving as factory hands, domestics, artisans, and construction workers.

Your Answer _____

_____

Correct Answers

A–82

White overseers directed black drivers, who supervised large groups of workers in the fields, all performing the same operation.

A–83

1) House slaves were spared harsh physical labor and enjoyed an intimate relationship with the owner's family.
2) They were deprived of social communion with other slaves, were many times viewed as traitors by other slaves, and had less privacy.

A–84

True

Q–85

How did the slave trade affect a slave's family unit?

Your Answer _____

_____

Q–86

When did the importation of slaves from abroad become illegal?

Your Answer _____

_____

Q–87

What did Gabriel Prosser, Denmark Vesey, and Nat Turner all have in common?

Your Answer _____

_____

Correct Answers

A–85

Families were frequently split apart.

A–86

1808

A–87

They all plotted or led uprisings of blacks against their white masters.

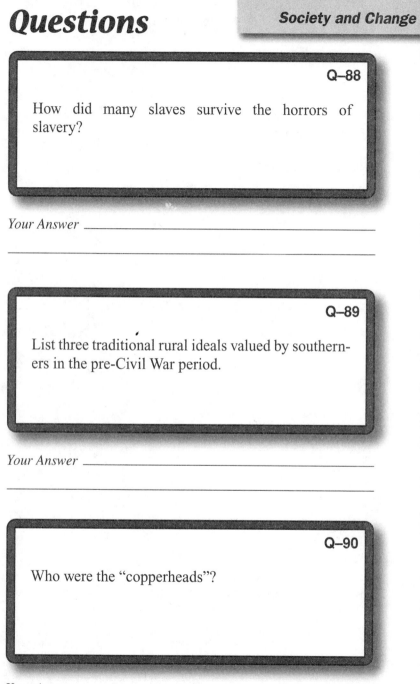

Q–88

How did many slaves survive the horrors of slavery?

Your Answer _____

_____

Q–89

List three traditional rural ideals valued by southerners in the pre-Civil War period.

Your Answer _____

_____

Q–90

Who were the "copperheads"?

Your Answer _____

_____

Correct Answers

A–88

They developed a distinctive network of tradition and interdependence.

A–89

Chivalry, leisure, and genteel elegance

A–90

Northerners opposed to the war

Questions

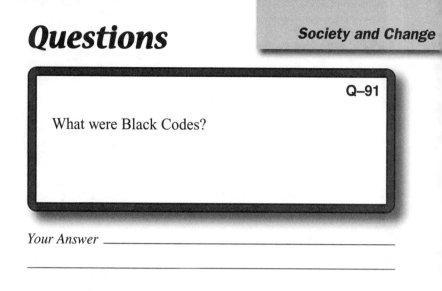

Q-91

What were Black Codes?

Your Answer _____

_____

Q-92

Who were the "carpetbaggers"?

Your Answer _____

_____

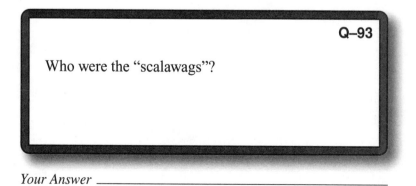

Q-93

Who were the "scalawags"?

Your Answer _____

_____

Correct Answers

A–91

Restrictions on the freedom of former slaves that were passed by southern states after the end of the Civil War

A–92

Northerners who came to the South to take part in Reconstruction governments

A–93

Southerners who supported Reconstruction governments

Q–94

What was the Ku Klux Klan and what was its purpose?

Your Answer _____

_____

Q–95

What were the staples that formed the southern diet in 1860?

Your Answer _____

_____

Q–96

About how many immigrants entered the United States during the 1870s? 1880s?

Your Answer _____

_____

Correct Answers

A–94

The Ku Klux Klan was an organization formed by southern whites that used violence to try to prevent blacks and white Republicans from voting.

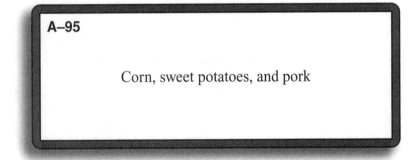

A–95

Corn, sweet potatoes, and pork

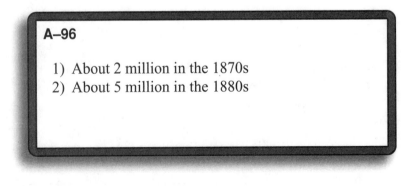

A–96

1) About 2 million in the 1870s
2) About 5 million in the 1880s

Questions

Q–97

How did the immigrants from the "old immigration" movement differ from those in the "new immigration" movement?

Your Answer _____

_____

Q–98

What two major problems did immigrants face during the 1880s?

Your Answer _____

_____

Q–99

What did immigrants obtain in exchange for giving political support to city governments?

Your Answer _____

_____

Correct Answers

A–97

The earlier immigrants came mostly from northern Europe, while the later immigrants came mostly from southern and eastern Europe.

A–98

Moving from one culture to another and moving from an agricultural environment to an industrial one

A–99

Jobs, housing, and social services

Questions

Q–100

Which two groups of immigrant workers fought for economic survival in California during the 1870s?

Your Answer _____

_____

Q–101

What was the "Gospel of Wealth"?

Your Answer _____

_____

Q–102

What was Social Darwinism?

Your Answer _____

_____

Correct Answers

A–100

The Irish and the Chinese

A–101

A belief held by rich people that wealth was a gift from God given to a select few

A–102

A philosophy of survival of the fittest

Questions

Q–103

What sociological theory developed during the 1880s in opposition to the Social Darwinian theory of genetic determinism?

Your Answer _____

Q–104

What farmers' organizations were formed after the Civil War?

Your Answer _____

Q–105

What happened to the nation's urban population between 1870 and 1900?

Your Answer _____

Correct Answers

A–103

The theory of the importance of intelligent planning
and decision making

A–104

The National Grange and the Farmers' Alliances

A–105

It doubled from 40 million to 80 million.

Questions

Q–106

What three cities each had a population of over 1 million by the year 1900?

Your Answer _____

_____

Q–107

What was the "social gospel"?

Your Answer _____

_____

Q–108

Who founded the Church of Christian Science?

Your Answer _____

_____

Correct Answers

A–106

New York, Chicago, and Philadelphia

A–107

Social gospel was a belief that settlement houses and better health and education services should be offered to immigrants.

A–108

Mary Baker Eddy

Questions

Q–109

What was the Salvation Army?

Your Answer _____

_____

Q–110

Who was Dwight Lyman Moody?

Your Answer _____

_____

Q–111

What were the three main purposes of settlement houses?

Your Answer _____

_____

Correct Answers

A–109

A religion founded in the 1870s

A–110

Dwight Lyman Moody was the leader of an urban revivalist movement during the 1880s.

A–111

The three main purposes were to settle poor immigrants, lobby against sweatshop labor conditions, and call for bans against child labor.

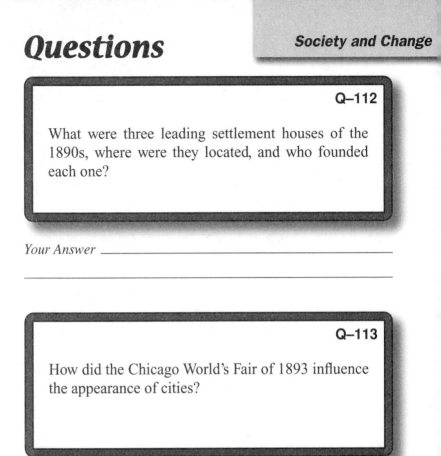

Q–112

What were three leading settlement houses of the 1890s, where were they located, and who founded each one?

Your Answer _____

_____

Q–113

How did the Chicago World's Fair of 1893 influence the appearance of cities?

Your Answer _____

_____

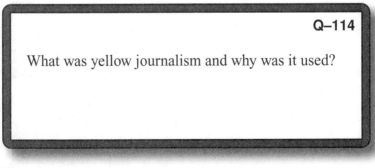

Q–114

What was yellow journalism and why was it used?

Your Answer _____

_____

Correct Answers

A–112

1) Hull House, Chicago, founded by Jane Addams
2) Henry Street Settlement, New York, founded by Lillian Wald
3) South End House, Boston, founded by Robert Archey Woods

A–113

The fair led to the expansion of urban public parks.

A–114

1) Yellow journalism was a policy of sensationalizing the news, particularly exaggerating atrocities in Cuba, followed by some newspapers.
2) It was used to increase circulation.

Questions

Q–115

What two newspapers took the lead in whipping up anti-Spanish feelings in 1898?

Your Answer _____

_____

Q–116

What was the Anti-Imperialist League?

Your Answer _____

_____

Q–117

How was the public mood affected by the First World War?

Your Answer _____

_____

Correct Answers

A–115

Joseph Pulitzer's *New York World* and William Randolph Hearst's *New York Journal*

A–116

The Anti-Imperialist League was an organization of Americans who opposed the United States's creating colonies out of territories it had captured from Spain.

A–117

A number of volunteer organizations sprang up around the country to search for draft dodgers, enforce the sale of bonds, and report any opinion or conversation considered suspicious. Organizations such as the American Protective League publicly humiliated people accused of not buying war bonds and persecuted, beat, and sometimes killed people of German descent.

Questions

Q–118

What was the major consequence of World War I for blacks and other racial minorities?

Your Answer _____

_____

Q–119

What was the primary reason for the Race Riots of 1919? In what city was rioting the worst?

Your Answer _____

_____

Q–120

How did World War I affect the Prohibition movement?

Your Answer _____

_____

Correct Answers

A–118

About half a million rural southern blacks migrated to cities, mainly in the North and Midwest, to obtain employment in war and other industries, especially in steel and meat packing.

A–119

1) White hostility based on competition for lower-paying jobs and black encroachment into white neighborhoods
2) The Chicago riot was the worst, lasting thirteen days and leaving 38 dead, 520 wounded, and 1,000 families homeless.

A–120

Proponents of Prohibition stressed the need for military personnel to be sober and the need to conserve grain for food.

Questions

Q–121

What was the first year that a majority of Americans lived in urban areas?

Your Answer _____

_____

Q–122

What explains the tremendous growth of the suburbs during the 1920s?

Your Answer _____

_____

Q–123

How did technology and urbanization lead to a sharp rise in the standard of living during the 1920s?

Your Answer _____

_____

Correct Answers

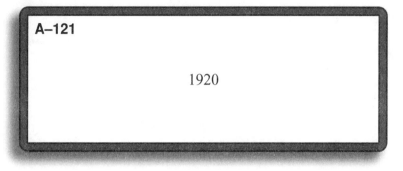

A–121

1920

A–122

Better transportation through streetcars, commuter railroads, and automobiles, as well as the easy availability of financing for home construction

A–123

Technological conveniences such as electric stoves, vacuum cleaners, refrigerators, washing machines, and toasters made life less burdensome. Urban living improved access to electricity, natural gas, telephones, and piped water.

Questions

Q–124

What were some of the characteristics of the "Jazz Age" of the 1920s?

Your Answer _____

_____

Q–125

What explains the growth of organized crime during the 1920s?

Your Answer _____

_____

Q–126

Who were Sacco and Vanzetti?

Your Answer _____

_____

Correct Answers

A–124

Greater sexual promiscuity, drinking, and new forms of dancing considered erotic by the older generation

A–125

Prohibition, because organized crime helped meet the demand for illegal alcohol

A–126

Sacco and Vanzetti were Italian immigrants and admitted anarchists convicted of murder in 1920 and sentenced to death. Many believe their convictions were based on the political radicalism of the defendants, not evidence.

Questions

Q–127

What spurred consumer interest and demand in the 1920s?

Your Answer _____

Q–128

How did the sexual revolution affect women's clothing in the 1920s?

Your Answer _____

Q–129

What was the only issue that united most Protestants in the 1920s?

Your Answer _____

Correct Answers

A–127

A great increase in professional advertising using newspapers, magazines, radio, billboards, and other media

A–128

Women adopted less bulky clothing, wearing short skirts and sleeveless and low-cut dresses.

A–129

Support for Prohibition

Questions

Q–130

What organization's membership growth in the 1920s was a reaction against the changing and modernizing American society?

Your Answer _____

_____

Q–131

Who was the most famous bootlegging gangster?

Your Answer _____

_____

Q–132

What was the American population by 1930?

Your Answer _____

_____

Correct Answers

A–130

Ku Klux Klan

A–131

Al Capone

A–132

Roughly 123 million

Q–133

What was the Bonus Army, why were they forced to leave Washington, and who commanded the force that removed them?

Your Answer _____

_____

Q–134

What were "Hoovervilles"?

Your Answer _____

_____

Q–135

Who was eligible to join the Civilian Conservation Corps? What kind of work did the Corps do?

Your Answer _____

_____

Correct Answers

A-133

1) The Bonus Army was a group of about 14,000 unemployed veterans who went to Washington in the summer of 1932 to lobby Congress for immediate payment of the bonus that had been approved in 1924 for payment in 1945.
2) After two veterans were killed in a clash with the police, President Herbert Hoover, calling them insurrectionists and communists, ordered the army to remove them.
3) General Douglas MacArthur

A-134

Makeshift shacks that housed hundreds of thousands of homeless people in empty spaces around cities during the Depression

A-135

1) Young men ages eighteen to twenty-four from families on relief
2) They worked on flood control, soil conservation, and forest projects under the direction of the War Department.

Questions

Q–136

What was the Tennessee Valley Authority (TVA)? What did the TVA represent?

Your Answer _____

_____

Q–137

Describe how the Works Progress Administration (WPA) worked.

Your Answer _____

_____

Q–138

What did the Rural Electrification Administration (REA) do?

Your Answer _____

_____

Correct Answers

A–136

1) The TVA, a public corporation under a three-member board, built twenty dams to stop flooding and soil erosion, improve navigation, and generate hydroelectric power.
2) The TVA represented the first major experiment in regional public planning.

A–137

The WPA employed people from the relief rolls for thirty hours of work a week at pay double the relief payment but less than private employment. Most of the projects undertaken were in construction.

A–138

The REA provided loans and WPA labor to electric cooperatives to build lines into rural areas not served by private companies.

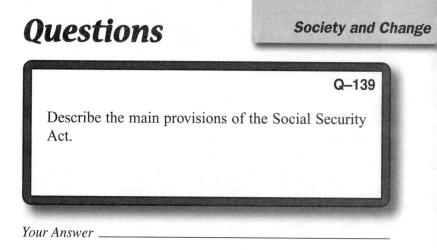

Q–139

Describe the main provisions of the Social Security Act.

Your Answer _____

_____

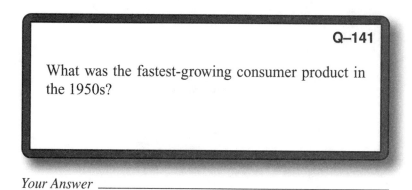

Q–140

What happened in the Rosenberg Case?

Your Answer _____

_____

Q–141

What was the fastest-growing consumer product in the 1950s?

Your Answer _____

_____

Correct Answers

A–139

The Social Security Act established a retirement plan for persons over age sixty-five funded by a tax or wages paid equally by employee and employer. The act also provided matching funds to the states for aid to the blind, handicapped, and dependent children.

A–140

In 1950, Julius and Ethel Rosenberg were charged with giving atomic secrets to the Soviet Union. They were convicted and executed in 1953.

A–141

Television

Questions

Q–142

Who pioneered the mass-produced housing development in the 1950s?

Your Answer _____

_____

Q–143

Who became an increasingly important consumer group during the 1950s?

Your Answer _____

_____

Q–144

What was the White Citizens' Council?

Your Answer _____

_____

Correct Answers

A–142

William Levitt

A–143

Teenagers

A–144

The White Citizens' Council was the leading organization throughout the South in resisting the *Brown v. Board of Education* decision.

Questions

Q–145

Explain the demographic trend called "white flight."

Your Answer _____

_____

Q–146

What was the role of women in society immediately after World War II?

Your Answer _____

_____

Q–147

By how much did home ownership grow between 1945 and 1960?

Your Answer _____

_____

Correct Answers

A–145

As blacks moved into the northern and midwestern cities, whites moved to the suburbs.

A–146

A cult of female domesticity re-emerged. Countless magazine articles promoted the concept that a woman's place was in the home.

A–147

50 percent

Questions

Q–148

How many Americans belonged to a church by 1960?

Your Answer _____

_____

Q–149

What was the difference between the counterculture and the New Left?

Your Answer _____

_____

Q–150

How many people were killed in the Watts riots in Los Angeles in 1965?

Your Answer _____

_____

Correct Answers

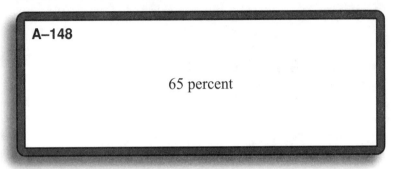

A–148

65 percent

A–149

Like the New Left, the founders of the counterculture were alienated by bureaucracy, materialism, and
the VietnamWar, but they turned away from politics
in favor of an alternative society.

A–150

Thirty-four

Questions

Q–151

What happened at Kent State University in May 1970?

Your Answer _____

_____

Q–152

What phrase was used to describe the 1970s generation?

Your Answer _____

_____

Q–153

What was the median age for Americans in 1980?

Your Answer _____

_____

Correct Answers

A–151

Four antiwar student protesters were killed by the National Guard.

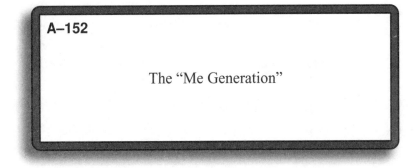

A–152

The "Me Generation"

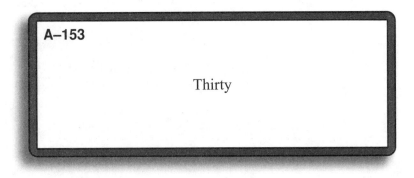

A–153

Thirty

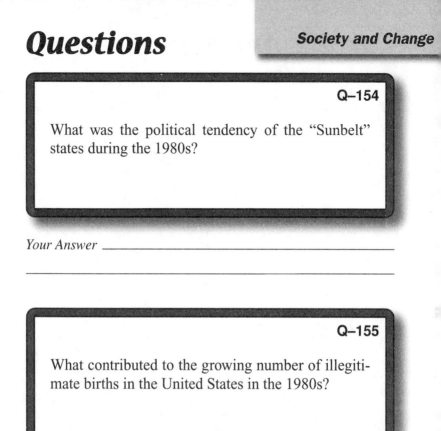

Q–154

What was the political tendency of the "Sunbelt" states during the 1980s?

Your Answer _____

_____

Q–155

What contributed to the growing number of illegitimate births in the United States in the 1980s?

Your Answer _____

_____

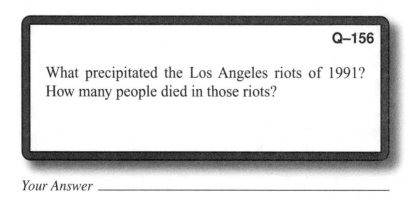

Q–156

What precipitated the Los Angeles riots of 1991? How many people died in those riots?

Your Answer _____

_____

Correct Answers

A–154

Conservative

A–155

The increased number of couples living together without getting married

A–156

1) The acquittal of Los Angeles police officers charged in the videotaped beating of Rodney King
2) Fifty-two

Q–157

What restriction on abortion was lifted by the Clinton administration in January of 1993?

Your Answer _____

_____

Q–158

What event started the Waco crisis in 1993? How did the crisis end?

Your Answer _____

_____

Q–159

Who was convicted of the 1993 World Trade Center bombing?

Your Answer _____

_____

Correct Answers

A–157

The "Gag Rule," which forbid discussion of abortion with patients at federally funded family planning clinics

A–158

1) In February 1993, the U.S. Bureau of Alcohol, Tobacco and Firearms raided the headquarters of the Branch Davidian religious cult near Waco, Texas, resulting in the killing of four federal agents.
2) After a fifty-one-day standoff, the FBI attacked the compound with tear gas and began destroying walls of the compound. Cult members apparently started a fire, resulting in the deaths of seventy-two Branch Davidians, including their leader David Koresh.

A–159

Four Arab terrorists

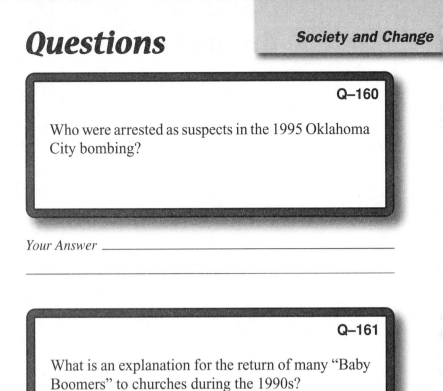

Q–160

Who were arrested as suspects in the 1995 Oklahoma City bombing?

Your Answer _____

_____

Q–161

What is an explanation for the return of many "Baby Boomers" to churches during the 1990s?

Your Answer _____

_____

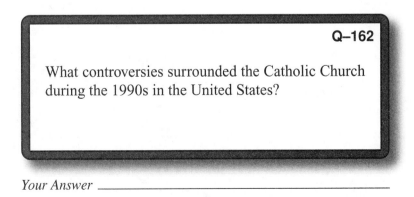

Q–162

What controversies surrounded the Catholic Church during the 1990s in the United States?

Your Answer _____

_____

Correct Answers

A–160

Two members of a right-wing, paramilitary militia

A–161

The increased family responsibilities of this group

A–162

Women in the priesthood, celibacy of priests, birth control, and abortion

Q–163

True or False: Before 1815, schools were primarily sponsored by private institutions.

Your Answer _____

_____

Q–164

What was the Lancastrian System?

Your Answer _____

_____

Q–165

Which nineteenth-century groups formed cooperative communities to improve the life of the common man against increasing industrialism?

Your Answer _____

_____

Correct Answers

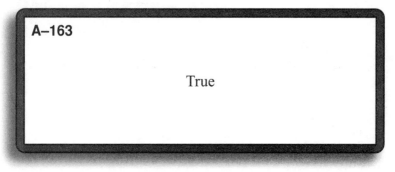

A–163

True

A–164

The Lancastrian System was an educational system in which older students tutored younger ones. The New York Free School experimented with this method for a time.

A–165

The Utopians

Questions

Q–166

Who founded the New Harmony, Indiana, commune?

Your Answer _____

_____

Q–167

Why did Owens's utopian community fail?

Your Answer _____

_____

Q–168

Who established the Nashoba Community in Memphis, Tennessee? How was it different from the other utopian communities of the nineteenth century?

Your Answer _____

_____

Correct Answers

A–166

Robert Owen

A–167

He encountered resistance from neighboring communities because he attacked religion, marriage, and the institution of property.

A–168

1) Robert Owen
2) It was a communal haven for freed slaves.

Questions

Q–169

Why did Alexis de Tocqueville travel to the United States to study the American prison system?

Your Answer _____

_____

Q–170

What was the name of the earliest commune in America?

Your Answer _____

_____

Q–171

What utopian community was based on free love and open marriage?

Your Answer _____

_____

Correct Answers

A–169

It was considered one of the most innovative in the world.

A–170

Brook Farm, Massachusetts

A–171

Oneida Community in New York

Questions

Q–172

What three practices did the Shakers follow?

Your Answer _____

Q–173

The _____ _____ in Iowa was a socialist experiment, with a rigidly ordered society.

Your Answer _____

Q–174

What group was the most successful of the communal experiments of the nineteenth century?

Your Answer _____

Correct Answers

A–172

Celibacy, sexual equality, and social discipline

A–173

Amana Community

A–174

The Mormons

Questions

Q–175

Who was Horace Mann?

Your Answer _____

_____

Q–176

Who was Dorothea Dix?

Your Answer _____

_____

Q–177

What was the purpose of the early antislavery movement?

Your Answer _____

_____

Correct Answers

A–175

Horace Mann was the first secretary of the Massachusetts Board of Education.

A–176

Dorothea Dix was a reformer who advocated for more humane treatment for the mentally incompetent in mental asylums.

A–177

The movement advocated the purchase and colonization of slaves.

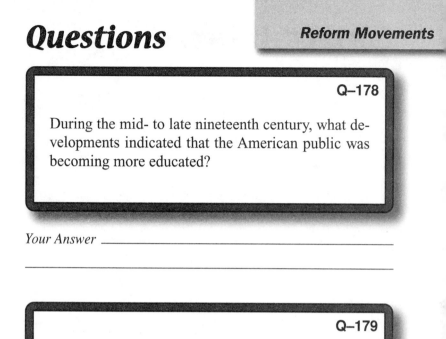

Q–178

During the mid- to late nineteenth century, what developments indicated that the American public was becoming more educated?

Your Answer _____

_____

Q–179

What were "booster colleges"?

Your Answer _____

_____

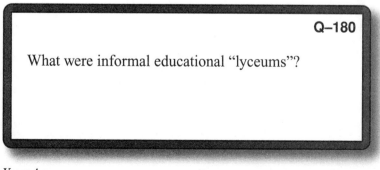

Q–180

What were informal educational "lyceums"?

Your Answer _____

_____

Correct Answers

A–178

A proliferation of newspapers and magazines and the springing up of new colleges indicated that the American public was becoming more educated.

A–179

These were colleges that sprang up in every new community as population moved west.

A–180

These were popular areas where the public could gather for cultural enrichment.

Questions

Q–181

What issues did the women's rights movement of the 1830s and 1840s focus upon?

Your Answer _____

_____

Q–182

Where and when did the first feminist meeting take place?

Your Answer _____

_____

Q–183

Why did the feminist movement suffer because of its link with the abolitionists?

Your Answer _____

_____

Correct Answers

A–181

Social and legal discrimination

A–182

Seneca Falls, New York, 1848

A–183

Feminism was considered of secondary importance to the abolitionist cause.

Questions

Q–184

Who was Sojourner Truth?

Your Answer _____

_____

Q–185

What was the Underground Railroad?

Your Answer _____

_____

Q–186

Who was Harriet Tubman?

Your Answer _____

_____

Correct Answers

A–184

Sojourner Truth was a well-known figure on the speakers' circuit who spoke against social and legal discrimination against women.

A–185

The Underground Railroad was a system by which northern abolitionists smuggled escaped slaves to permanent freedom in Canada.

A–186

Harriet Tubman was one of the main operators of the Underground Railroad, leading over 300 of her friends and family to freedom after she had escaped slavery.

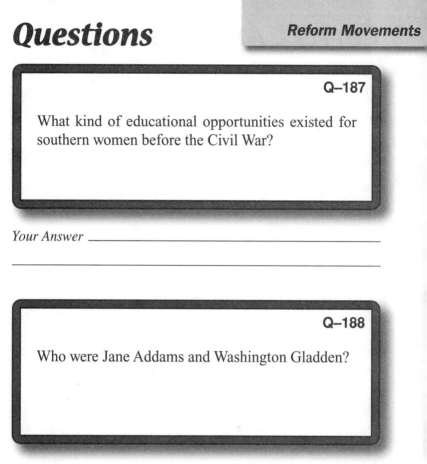

Q–187

What kind of educational opportunities existed for southern women before the Civil War?

Your Answer _____

_____

Q–188

Who were Jane Addams and Washington Gladden?

Your Answer _____

_____

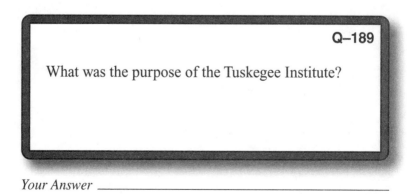

Q–189

What was the purpose of the Tuskegee Institute?

Your Answer _____

_____

Correct Answers

A–187

Education for southern women was rare; what little there was centered on the "domestic arts."

A–188

Advocates of the "social gospel"

A–189

To provide teaching and vocational education for African Americans

Questions

Q–190

Who became president of the Tuskegee Institute in 1881?

Your Answer _____

Q–191

Why did feminism become stronger during the 1870s and 1880s?

Your Answer _____

Q–192

What educational innovation did Johns Hopkins University pioneer in the 1880s?

Your Answer _____

Correct Answers

A–190

Booker T. Washington

A–191

Because millions of women worked outside the home and were active in social reform movements

A–192

Graduate seminars

Questions

Q–193

What four women's colleges were established in the 1880s?

Your Answer _____

_____

Q–194

Who was Jacob Coxey?

Your Answer _____

_____

Q–195

What was the relationship between the Depression of 1893 and the formation of the Anti-Saloon League?

Your Answer _____

_____

Correct Answers

A–193

Bryn Mawr, Vassar, Wellesley, and Mount Holyoke

A–194

Jacob Coxey was a Populist businessman who led a march of unemployed workers to Washington to petition for a government work relief program.

A–195

High unemployment caused by the depression led to increased drunkenness by male workers, which in turn led women to support an anti-saloon movement.

Questions

Q–196

What educational development grew out of the Chautauqua Movement?

Your Answer _____

_____

Q–197

Who wrote *How the Other Half Lives*? What did the author criticize?

Your Answer _____

_____

Q–198

What three kinds of political reforms took place at the state level during the early 1900s?

Your Answer _____

_____

Correct Answers

A–196

Home study courses

A–197

1) Jacob Riis
2) Riis criticized the poverty, illness, crime, and despair of New York's slums.

A–198

Primary elections, initiative and referendum, and the rooting out of political machines

---

Questions

Q–199

Who was Robert LaFollette?

Your Answer _____

_____

Q–200

What did the National Association for the Advancement of Colored People advocate?

Your Answer _____

_____

Q–201

Who was W. E. B. DuBois?

Your Answer _____

_____

Correct Answers

A–199

Robert LaFollette was a leading reformer in Wisconsin during the early 1900s.

A–200

An end to racial segregation

A–201

W. E. B. DuBois was an African American intellectual militant who founded the Niagara Movement.

Questions

Q–202

What did the Niagara Movement want the federal government to do?

Your Answer _____

_____

Q–203

Who were the muckrakers?

Your Answer _____

_____

Q–204

What were some popular muckraking magazines of the early 1900s?

Your Answer _____

_____

Correct Answers

A–202

Pass laws to protect racial equality and full rights of citizenship for African Americans

A–203

The muckrackers were investigative journalists and authors who favored progressive political, economic, and social reforms in the early 1900s.

A–204

McClure's, Collier's, Cosmopolitan, and *Everybody's*

Questions

Q–205

Who was Ida Tarbell?

Your Answer _____

_____

Q–206

Who was Lincoln Steffens?

Your Answer _____

_____

Q–207

What types of reforms did the Bull Moose Party stand for in 1912?

Your Answer _____

_____

Correct Answers

A–205

Ida Tarbell was the muckraking author of *History of Standard Oil Company.*

A–206

Lincoln Steffens was the muckraking author of *Shame of the Cities.*

A–207

Women's suffrage, direct election of senators, presidential primaries, and the abolition of child labor

Questions

Q–208

Who were the Wobblies?

Your Answer _____

Q–209

Who was Horace Greeley?

Your Answer _____

Q–210

What ideas are associated with Marcus Garvey?

Your Answer _____

Correct Answers

A–208

The Wobblies were members of a radical labor organization called the Industrial Workers of the World (I.W.W.). In the early 1900s, this organization was successful in the textile industry and the western mining industry.

A–209

Horace Greeley was founder and editor of the *New York Tribune*.

A–210

Marcus Garvey advocated black racial pride, separatism, and a return of blacks to Africa rather than integration.

Questions

Q–211

Why was President Franklin D. Roosevelt reluctant to support antilynching legislation?

Your Answer _____

_____

Q–212

What did the Civil Rights Act of 1957 establish?

Your Answer _____

_____

Q–213

Who were the "Freedom Riders"?

Your Answer _____

_____

Correct Answers

A–211

He was fearful of alienating the southern wing of the Democratic Party.

A–212

The Civil Rights Act of 1957 established a permanent Civil Rights Commission and a Civil Rights Division of the Justice Department that was empowered to prevent interference with the right to vote.

A–213

The Freedom Riders were a group of blacks and whites who traveled across the South in 1961 to test federal enforcement of regulations prohibiting discrimination.

Questions

Q–214

What was the 1963 March on Washington?

Your Answer _____

_____

Q–215

Name the most important provisions of the 1964 Civil Rights Act.

Your Answer _____

_____

Q–216

What important education bill was passed in 1965?

Your Answer _____

_____

Correct Answers

A–214

The 1963 March on Washington was a demonstration by over 200,000 people in support of the 1963 Civil Rights Bill. It was at this demonstration that Martin Luther King, Jr., gave his famous "I Have a Dream" speech.

A–215

The 1964 Civil Rights Act outlawed racial discrimination by employers and unions, created the Equal Employment Opportunity Commission to enforce the law, and eliminated the remaining restrictions on black voting.

A–216

The Elementary and Secondary Education Act, which provided $1.5 billion to school districts to improve the education of poor people

Questions

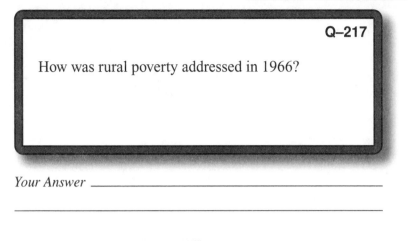

Q–217

How was rural poverty addressed in 1966?

Your Answer _____

_____

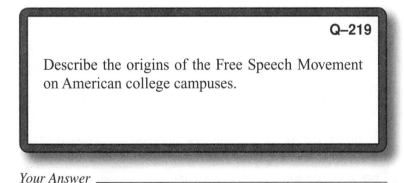

Q–218

What was the conclusion of the Kerner Commission about the cause of the racial riots of the 1960s?

Your Answer _____

_____

Q–219

Describe the origins of the Free Speech Movement on American college campuses.

Your Answer _____

_____

Correct Answers

A–217

The Appalachian Regional Development Act of 1966 provided $1.1 billion for isolated mountain areas.

A–218

The Kerner Commission concluded that the riots were directed at a social system that prevented blacks from getting good jobs and crowded them into ghettos.

A–219

Students at the University of California, Berkeley, staged sit-ins in 1964 to protest the prohibition of political canvassing on campus. Led by Mario Savio, the movement changed from emphasizing student rights to criticizing the bureaucracy of American society.

Q–220

What was the leading New Left student group during the 1960s?

Your Answer _____

_____

Q–221

What did the 1991 Civil Rights Act establish?

Your Answer _____

_____

Q–222

What report precipitated a crisis in education during the 1980s?

Your Answer _____

_____

Correct Answers

A–220

Students for a Democratic Society (SDS)

A–221

The 1991 Civil Rights Act required employers in discrimination suits to prove that their hiring practices were not discriminatory.

A–222

A 1981 report called "A Nation at Risk," prepared by the National Commission of Excellence in Education, argued that a "rising tide of mediocrity" characterized the nation's schools.

Q–223

How did states respond to the educational crisis of the 1980s?

Your Answer _____

_____

Q–224

What was the name of the leading suffrage movement in the early twentieth century?

Your Answer _____

_____

Q–225

Who founded the Share Our Wealth Society in 1934?

Your Answer _____

_____

Correct Answers

A–223

Many states instituted reforms including higher teacher salaries, competency tests for teachers, and an increase in required subjects for high school graduation.

A–224

The National American Woman Suffrage Association

A–225

Senator Huey Long of Louisiana

Questions

Q–226

Who was the leader of the National Union for Social Justice?

Your Answer _____

_____

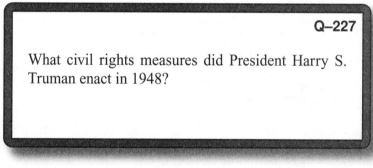

Q–227

What civil rights measures did President Harry S. Truman enact in 1948?

Your Answer _____

_____

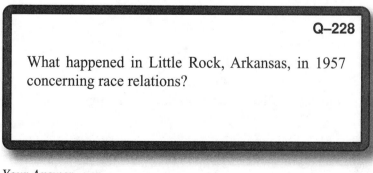

Q–228

What happened in Little Rock, Arkansas, in 1957 concerning race relations?

Your Answer _____

_____

Correct Answers

A–226

Father Charles E. Coughlin

A–227

He banned racial discrimination in federal government hiring practices and ordered the desegregation of the armed forces.

A–228

President Dwight D. Eisenhower sent 10,000 National Guardsmen and 1,000 paratroopers to control mobs and enable blacks to enroll in Central High School.

Questions

Q–229

What is Rosa Parks famous for?

Your Answer _____

_____

Q–230

Why did President John F. Kennedy send the National Guard into Mississippi in the fall of 1962?

Your Answer _____

_____

Q–231

Who were the two leading figures in the Black Power movement during the 1960s?

Your Answer _____

_____

Correct Answers

A–229

Rosa Parks's arrest on December 11, 1955, was a catalyst for the civil rights movement. She was arrested for refusing to give up her seat on a bus to a white passenger.

A–230

To ensure that a black student, James Meredith, could enroll at the University of Mississippi

A–231

Stokely Carmichael and H. Rap Brown

Q–232

What was a common criticism of universities by student protesters during the 1960s?

Your Answer _____

_____

Q–233

What split the antiwar movement during the 1960s?

Your Answer _____

_____

Q–234

What was the class origin of the women's movement?

Your Answer _____

_____

Correct Answers

A–232

The common criticism was bureaucracies were indifferent to students' needs.

A–233

It split between those favoring violence and those opposed to it.

A–234

The women's movement was largely limited to the middle class.

Questions

Q–235

What event was a catalyst for the gay rights movement?

Your Answer _____

Q–236

What was the name of the militant antiabortion group that became active during the early 1990s?

Your Answer _____

Culture, Art, and Literature

Q–237

The eighteenth-century European intellectual movement is known as the _____.

Your Answer _____

Correct Answers

A–235

A police raid in 1969 on the Stonewall Inn, a gay hangout in the Greenwich Village section of New York City

A–236

Operation Rescue

A–237

Enlightenment

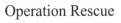 **Take Test-Readiness Quiz 1 on CD**
(to review questions 1–237)

Q–238

_____ _____, an English political Enlightenment philosopher, advocated the overthrow of government that abuses the subjects' rights of life, liberty, and property.

Your Answer _____

Q–239

Who wrote *Poor Richard's Almanac*?

Your Answer _____

Q–240

Who wrote the pamphlet *"Common Sense"*? Why was it so important?

Your Answer _____

Correct Answers

A–238

John Locke

A–239

Benjamin Franklin

A–240

1) Thomas Paine
2) It was widely sold and had a great deal of influence in urging Americans to achieve independence
from Britain.

Q–241

What event inspired Francis Scott Key to write *"The Star-Spangled Banner"*?

Your Answer _____

Q–242

What nineteenth-century American author is best remembered for his portraits of Hudson River characters?

Your Answer _____

Q–243

Alexis de Tocqueville's book, _____, published in 1835, reflected a broad interest in the entire spectrum of the American democratic process and the society in which it developed.

Your Answer _____

Correct Answers

A–241

The holding firm of Fort McHenry against British bombardment during the invasion of Chesapeake Bay

A–242

Washington Irving

A–243

Democracy in America

Questions

Q-244

The _____ movement of the nineteenth century emphasized the emotions and feelings over rationality.

Your Answer _____

Q-245

What famous nineteenth-century author wrote *Leatherstocking Tales*?

Your Answer _____

Q-246

Which famous nineteenth-century author wrote *Leaves of Grass*?

Your Answer _____

Correct Answers

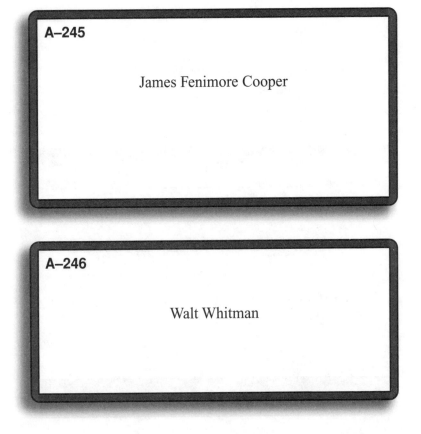

A–244

Romanticism

A–245

James Fenimore Cooper

A–246

Walt Whitman

Questions

Q–247

The epic poems *Evangeline* and *Hiawatha* were written by _____ _____ _____.

Your Answer _____

Q–248

True or False: *Moby-Dick, Typee,* and *Billy Budd* were written by Nathaniel Hawthorne.

Your Answer _____

Q–249

_____ _____ _____ by Francis Parkman described the opening frontier of the Rocky Mountains and beyond.

Your Answer _____

Correct Answers

A–247

Henry Wadsworth Longfellow

A–248

False. Herman Melville was the author.

A–249

The Oregon Trail

Questions

Q–250

Who wrote the *Bigelow Papers* and *Commemorative Ode?*

Your Answer _____

Q–251

_____ _____ wrote of Puritan bigotry in *The Scarlet Letter.*

Your Answer _____

Q–252

Who authored "*The Raven*" and other tales of terror and darkness?

Your Answer _____

Correct Answers

A–250

James Russell Lowell

A–251

Nathaniel Hawthorne

A–252

Edgar Allan Poe

Q–253

What nineteenth-century South Carolina poet defended the slave system and the southern way of life?

Your Answer _____

Q–254

_____ _____, a Georgia storyteller, used earthy and vulgar language to depict common southern folk.

Your Answer _____

Q–255

Which nineteenth-century Hudson River School artist painted a wide array of American birds and animals?

Your Answer _____

Correct Answers

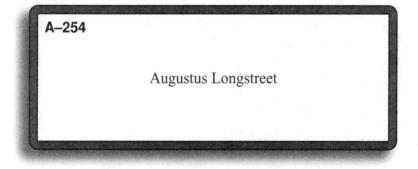

A–253

William Gilmore Simms

A–254

Augustus Longstreet

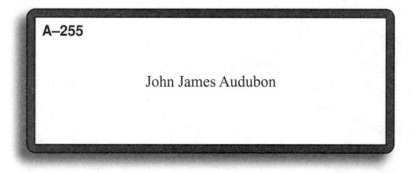

A–255

John James Audubon

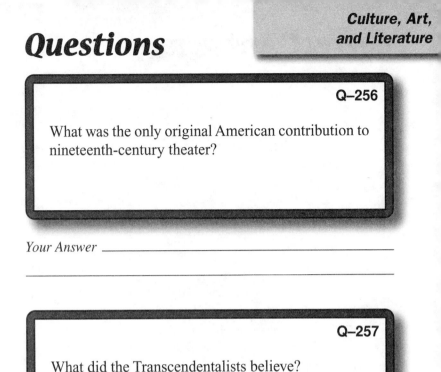

Q–256

What was the only original American contribution to nineteenth-century theater?

Your Answer _____

Q–257

What did the Transcendentalists believe?

Your Answer _____

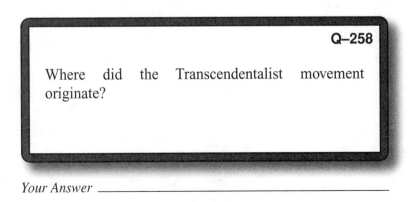

Q–258

Where did the Transcendentalist movement originate?

Your Answer _____

Correct Answers

A–256

The blackface minstrel show

A–257

Their objective was to transcend the intellect and strive for emotional understanding to attain unity with God.

A–258

Concord, Massachusetts

Q–259

Who authored *"Nature"* and *"Self-Reliance"*?

Your Answer _____

Q–260

Who was John L. O'Sullivan?

Your Answer _____

Q–261

Who authored *Walden* and *Civil Disobedience*, rejected the repression of society, and preached civil disobedience to protest unjust laws?

Your Answer _____

Correct Answers

A–259

Ralph Waldo Emerson

A–260

John L. O'Sullivan was a New York journalist who coined the phrase "manifest destiny."

A–261

Henry David Thoreau

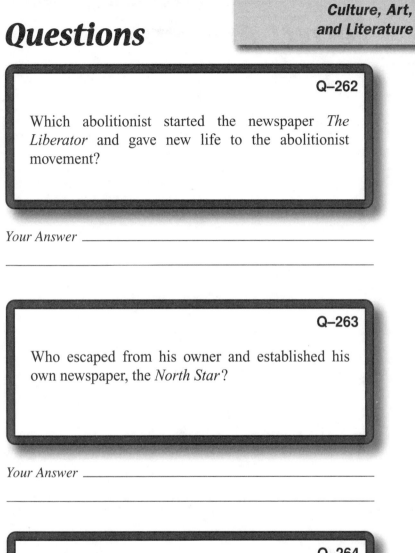

Q–262

Which abolitionist started the newspaper *The Liberator* and gave new life to the abolitionist movement?

Your Answer _____

_____

Q–263

Who escaped from his owner and established his own newspaper, the *North Star*?

Your Answer _____

_____

Q–264

What were "penny press" papers?

Your Answer _____

_____

Correct Answers

A–262

William Lloyd Garrison

A–263

Frederick Douglass

A–264

The penny press papers were inexpensive newspapers that appealed to a larger audience by offering simply but vividly written news and human interest stories at a cheap price: a penny per paper.

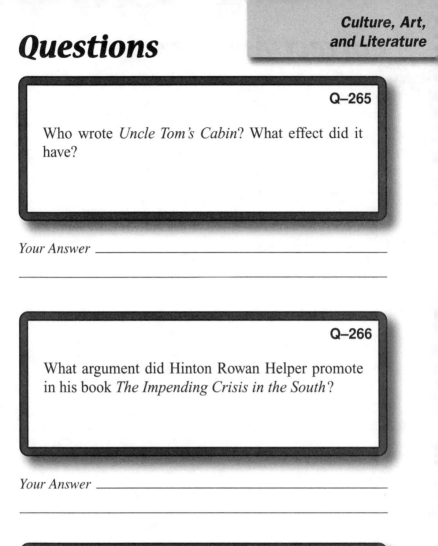

Q–265

Who wrote *Uncle Tom's Cabin*? What effect did it have?

Your Answer _____

_____

Q–266

What argument did Hinton Rowan Helper promote in his book *The Impending Crisis in the South*?

Your Answer _____

_____

Q–267

What qualities did the Horatio Alger stories promote?

Your Answer _____

_____

Correct Answers

A–265

1) Harriet Beecher Stowe
2) It made many northerners active opponents of slavery and created sympathy for the North with the British public.

A–266

Helper argued that slavery was harmful to the South and that it enriched the large planter at the expense of the small independent farmer.

A–267

Hard work and honesty

Q–268

Who was Mark Twain?

Your Answer _____

_____

Q–269

What was the "Greatest Show on Earth"?

Your Answer _____

_____

Q–270

What kind of literature and art gradually replaced Romanticism during the 1880s?

Your Answer _____

_____

Correct Answers

A–268

Mark Twain was a famous author of the late nineteenth to early twentieth century whose works include *The Adventures of Tom Sawyer* and *The Gilded Age.*

A–269

The Barnum and Bailey Circus

A–270

Realism

Q–271

What are two books written by Henry James?

Your Answer _____

_____

Q–272

Who wrote *A Century of Dishonor*?

Your Answer _____

_____

Q–273

What were the "Br'er Rabbit Tales"? What other literary character did Joel Chandler Harris develop?

Your Answer _____

_____

Correct Answers

A–272

Helen Hunt Jackson

A–273

1) The "Br'er Rabbit Tales" were an oral literature that developed among slaves in which they secretly ridiculed their masters.
2) Uncle Remus

Questions

Q–274

What was the thesis of Josiah Strong's book *Our Country*?

Your Answer _____

_____

Q–275

To what category of literature did Edward Bellamy's book *Looking Backward* belong?

Your Answer _____

_____

Q–276

What was the significance of William James's book *Principles of Psychology*?

Your Answer _____

_____

Correct Answers

A–274

Americans had a mission to export the word of God around the world, especially to nonwhite populations.

A–275

Science fiction

A–276

It introduced American readers to the modern science of psychology.

Questions

Q–277

Who was Captain Alfred Thayer Mahan?

Your Answer _____

_____

Q–278

Who was Joseph Pulitzer?

Your Answer _____

_____

Q–279

Who wrote *Maggie: A Girl of the Streets* and *The Red Badge of Courage*?

Your Answer _____

_____

Correct Answers

A–277

Captain Alfred Thayer Mahan was an author who wrote *The Influence of Seapower on History, 1660–1783*, which argued that control of the seas was the means to world power.

A–278

Joseph Pulitzer was the first newspaper publisher to reach a mass audience of more than 100,000 readers with his New York *World*.

A–279

Stephen Crane

Q–280

Who wrote *Theory of the Leisure Class* and what did he criticize?

Your Answer _____

_____

Q–281

What did Theodore Dreiser, Upton Sinclair, and Jack London have in common?

Your Answer _____

_____

Q–282

Where did the silent film industry start?

Your Answer _____

_____

Correct Answers

A–280

Thorstein Veblen was the author; he criticized the "conspicuous consumption" of the leisure class.

A–281

All three authors wrote novels with a social message during the early 1900s.

A–282

It started in New York and New Jersey.

Questions

Q–283

What were the main points of Woodrow Wilson's book *Congressional Government*?

Your Answer _____

_____

Q–284

What movie embodied the racist feelings in America during the 1910s and 1920s and is also important due to its technical achievements?

Your Answer _____

_____

Q–285

What two popular forms of music were developed primarily by black musicians during the 1920s?

Your Answer _____

_____

Correct Answers

A–283

Wilson criticized the committee system in Congress and called for closer cooperation between the executive and legislative branches of government.

A–284

The Birth of a Nation (1915)

A–285

Jazz and blues

Q–286

What sports celebrity became a cultural icon during the 1920s and helped make baseball America's sport?

Your Answer _____

_____

Q–287

Whose solo flight across the Atlantic in 1927 captured the world's imagination and made people feel that anything was possible?

Your Answer _____

_____

Q–288

When was sound introduced to motion pictures? What was the name of the first feature-length motion picture that offered sound?

Your Answer _____

_____

Correct Answers

A–286

Babe Ruth

A–287

Charles Lindbergh

A–288

1) 1927
2) *The Jazz Singer*

Questions

Q–289

What was the most popular form of music in the 1930s?

Your Answer _____

_____

Q–290

Explain the term "Lost Generation."

Your Answer _____

_____

Q–291

What was the effect of radio on American culture?

Your Answer _____

_____

Correct Answers

A–289

Swing or big band music

A–290

The "Lost Generation" refers to the many talented writers of the 1920s who were disgusted with the hypocrisy and materialism of contemporary American society. Members of this group of writers include Ernest Hemingway, F. Scott Fitzgerald, Ezra Pound, and T. S. Eliot.

A–291

It tended to make Americans more uniform in their attitudes, taste, speech, and humor.

Q–292

Identify the 1940 movie classic that commented on the Depression.

Your Answer _____

_____

Q–293

What was the theme of Arthur Miller's *Death of a Salesman*? When was it written?

Your Answer _____

_____

Q–294

Who were the Beats?

Your Answer _____

_____

Correct Answers

A–292

The Grapes of Wrath

A–293

1) The loneliness of the externally directed person
2) 1949

A–294

The Beats were a group of young writers in the 1950s alienated by twentieth-century life who emphasized alcohol, drugs, sex, jazz, and Buddhism.

Q–295

Who wrote *The Feminine Mystique* in 1963? What was the main point of the book?

Your Answer _____

_____

Q–296

How did the recording industry respond in 1990 to conservative attacks on "indecency" in the entertainment industry?

Your Answer _____

_____

Q–297

Who became the first woman to win the Nobel Prize for literature in 1993?

Your Answer _____

_____

Correct Answers

A–295

1) Betty Friedan
2) That middle-class society stifled women and did not allow them to use their individual talents

A–296

By agreeing to place new uniform warning labels on recordings that contained potentially offensive language

A–297

Toni Morrison

Q–298

What controversy surrounded the National Endowment for the Arts (NEA) in 1989?

Your Answer _____

_____

Growth of the American Political System

Q–299

In 1620, before going ashore, the Pilgrims drew up the _____ _____, which established an orderly government based on the consent of the governed.

Your Answer _____

_____

Q–300

How did the Virginia gentry respond to Britain's tightening of their local autonomy?

Your Answer _____

_____

Correct Answers

A–298

The NEA was accused of using federal money to support "obscene or indecent projects."

A–299

Mayflower Compact

A–300

They used political means to block the governor's efforts to increase royal control.

Questions

Q–301

What was the first representative assembly in the New World?

Your Answer _____

_____

Q–302

In which colony was the first constitution written? What was it called?

Your Answer _____

_____

Q–303

After the *Gaspee* incident, Americans formed _____ _____ _____ to communicate with other colonies regarding possible threats from the British government.

Your Answer _____

_____

Correct Answers

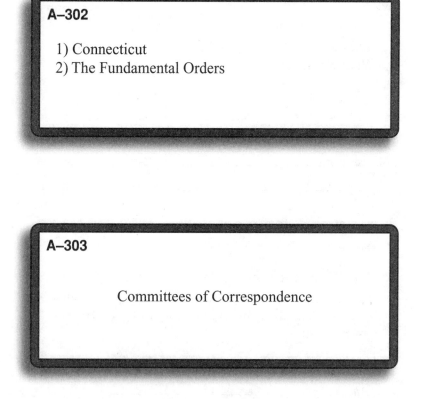

A–301

The House of Burgesses

A–302

1) Connecticut
2) The Fundamental Orders

A–303

Committees of Correspondence

Q–304

What two main factions existed at the Second Continental Congress?

Your Answer _____

Q–305

What three resolves were undertaken by the Second Continental Congress to deal with the divisive factions in the colonies?

Your Answer _____

Q–306

On June 7, 1776, _____ _____ _____ of Virginia introduced a series of formal resolutions in Congress, calling for independence and a national government.

Your Answer _____

Correct Answers

A–304

1) New Englanders who leaned toward declaring independence from Britain
2) A group, led by John Dickinson of Pennsylvania, which drew its strength from the middle colonies and was not yet ready to declare its independence

A–305

1) It adopted a New England army based near Boston and urged other colonies to send additional troops under George Washington's command.
2) It adopted a "Declaration of Causes and Necessity for Taking up Arms."
3) It pleaded with King George in an "Olive Branch Petition" to restore peace by interceding with Parliament.

A–306

Richard Henry Lee

Questions

Q–307

What was the Declaration of Independence?

Your Answer _____

_____

Q–308

True or False: Most of the original state constitutions included a bill of rights.

Your Answer _____

_____

Q–309

The first document that devised a framework for the national government of the United States was known as the _____ _____ _____.

Your Answer _____

_____

Correct Answers

A–307

Written largely by Thomas Jefferson and adopted on July 4, 1776, the Declaration of Independence explained to Parliament, loyalists, and the rest of the world why America was justified to separate from Great Britain.

A–308

True

A–309

Articles of Confederation

Q–310

What powers did America's first constitution, the Articles of Confederation, grant the federal government? What was not allowed?

Your Answer _____

_____

Q–311

What were the most important and longest-lasting pieces of legislation during the Articles of Confederation government?

Your Answer _____

_____

Q–312

What did Shay's Rebellion indicate to many Americans?

Your Answer _____

_____

Correct Answers

A–310

The Articles of Confederation created a weak federal government that allowed the federal government to make war and foreign policies, but it did not allow the national government to levy taxes, raise troops, or regulate trade.

A–311

The Land Ordinance of 1785 divided the western lands into townships, allowing for one section of land to be used for public education. The Northwest Ordinance of 1787 created the Northwest Territory and banned slavery there.

A–312

Shay's Rebellion alerted Americans that a stronger central government was needed to control violent uprisings.

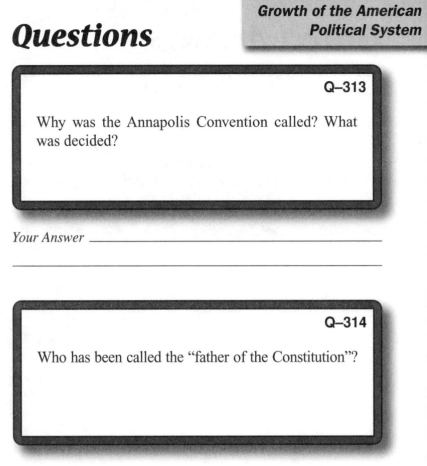

Q–313

Why was the Annapolis Convention called? What was decided?

Your Answer _____

_____

Q–314

Who has been called the "father of the Constitution"?

Your Answer _____

_____

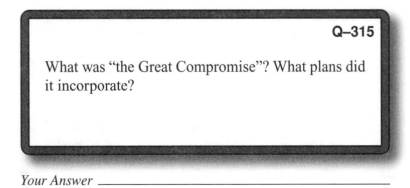

Q–315

What was "the Great Compromise"? What plans did it incorporate?

Your Answer _____

_____

Correct Answers

A–313

1) The Annapolis Convention was called to discuss problems regarding interstate commerce under the Articles of Confederation.
2) Delegates decided to call a convention of all states to revise the Articles of Confederation.

A–314

James Madison

A–315

The Great Compromise was the agreement reached at the Constitutional Convention of 1787 that established the federal government's bicameral legislature: a Senate in which each state was represented by two senators (New Jersey Plan), and a House of Representatives based on population (Virginia Plan).

Questions

Q–316

What were the main tenets of the Three-Fifths Compromise?

Your Answer _____

Q–317

What power was granted to the president that allowed him to check Congress?

Your Answer _____

Q–318

Which branch has the power to impeach the president or other high government officials?

Your Answer _____

Correct Answers

A–316

1) Each slave would count as three-fifths of a person for purposes of taxation and representation.
2) The federal government was prohibited from stopping the importation of slaves prior to 1808.

A–317

The power to veto Congress's legislation

A–318

The legislative branch or Congress

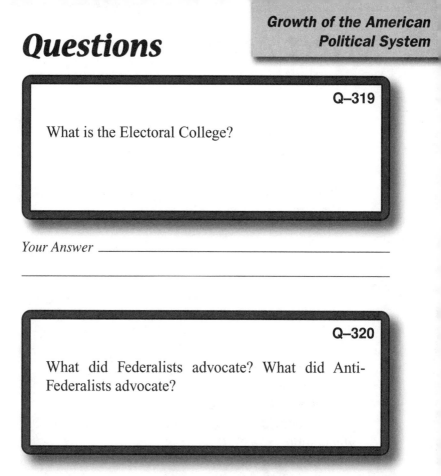

Q–319

What is the Electoral College?

Your Answer _____

_____

Q–320

What did Federalists advocate? What did Anti-Federalists advocate?

Your Answer _____

_____

Q–321

What were "The Federalist Papers"?

Your Answer _____

_____

Correct Answers

A–319

The Electoral College is a body of electors from each state, based on the state's combined number of senators and representatives. Its function is to elect the president.

A–320

1) Federalists advocated a strong centralized government and endorsed the Constitution.
2) Anti-Federalists advocated stronger states' rights and endorsed amending the Articles of Confederation.

A–321

The papers were written as a series of eighty-five newspaper articles by Alexander Hamilton, John Jay, and James Madison. They expounded the virtues of the Constitution.

Questions

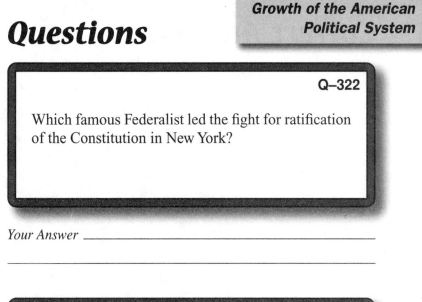

Q–322

Which famous Federalist led the fight for ratification of the Constitution in New York?

Your Answer _____

_____

Q–323

What is the Bill of Rights?

Your Answer _____

_____

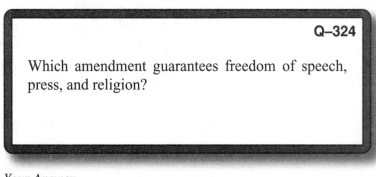

Q–324

Which amendment guarantees freedom of speech, press, and religion?

Your Answer _____

_____

Correct Answers

A–322

Alexander Hamilton

A–323

The Bill of Rights is the first ten amendments to the Constitution, which embody guarantees of personal liberties for Americans.

A–324

The First Amendment

Q–325

Which amendment grants to states those powers not granted to the federal government?

Your Answer _____

_____

Q–326

What was the Judiciary Act of 1789?

Your Answer _____

_____

Q–327

Why did Thomas Jefferson object to Alexander Hamilton's funding of the national debt at face value?

Your Answer _____

_____

Correct Answers

A–325

The Tenth Amendment

A–326

The Judiciary Act of 1789 provided for a federal court system and a Supreme Court consisting of six justices, and created jurisdictions for the federal courts.

A–327

Jefferson believed that Hamilton's proposal would benefit speculators who had bought up state and confederation obligations at depressed prices.

Questions

Q–328

What is a broad interpretation of the Constitution?

Your Answer _____

_____

Q–329

Thomas Jefferson and James Madison, who opposed Alexander Hamilton's Bank of the United States, came to be known as _____ _____.

Your Answer _____

_____

Q–330

Which groups supported the Federalists?

Your Answer _____

_____

Correct Answers

A–328

Advocates of a strong central government claimed that the government was given "implied powers" or all powers not expressly denied to it.

A–329

Democrat Republicans

A–330

Business and financial groups in commercial centers of the Northeast and the port cities of the South

Questions

Q–331

What areas of the country supported Thomas Jefferson and the Republicans?

Your Answer _____

_____

Q–332

What was the Whiskey Rebellion? How did President George Washington respond to it?

Your Answer _____

_____

Q–333

Why were the Alien and Sedition Acts of 1798 passed?

Your Answer _____

_____

Correct Answers

A–331

The rural areas of the South and West

A–332

1) A group of Pennsylvania farmers refused to pay the excise tax on whiskey and also terrorized tax collectors.
2) President Washington sent 15,000 federal troops to crush the rebellion and to display the dominance of the federal government.

A–333

To stifle actual or potential Democrat Republican opposition to the Federalist-controlled government during the "undeclared war" with France

Questions

Q–334

What were the Kentucky and Virginia Resolves?

Your Answer _____

Q–335

How did John Adams guarantee continuation of Federalist policies after his presidency?

Your Answer _____

Q–336

List four actions taken by the Jefferson administration that reversed former Federalist policies.

Your Answer _____

Correct Answers

A–334

These were a series of resolves drawn up by Thomas Jefferson and James Madison that were presented to the Kentucky and Virginia legislatures; they proposed that John Locke's compact theory should be applied. This would nullify federal laws in those states.

A–335

By filling positions, many newly created, with party supporters such as John Marshall. Many of these appointments occurred right at the end of his presidency and are thus referred to as "midnight judges."

A–336

1) Suspended enforcement of the Alien and Sedition Acts
2) Reduced the size of the federal bureaucracy
3) Repealed excise taxes
4) Reduced the size of the army

Questions

Q–337

What controversies did Aaron Burr become involved in during his political career?

Your Answer _____

Q–338

What was the Essex Junto of 1804?

Your Answer _____

Q–339

Henry Clay, John C. Calhoun, and other strong prowar Congressmen became known as _____ _____.

Your Answer _____

Correct Answers

A–337

Election of 1800; killing Alexander Hamilton in a duel; the Essex Junto; and the Burr Conspiracy to take Mexico from Spain and establish a new nation

A–338

Some New England Federalists saw western expansion as a threat to their position in the union and moved to organize a secessionist movement.

A–339

War Hawks

Q–340

What resolutions were drafted by the New England delegates at the Hartford Convention in December 1814?

Your Answer _____

_____

Q–341

Why may it be said that the election of James Monroe in 1817 indicated national unity?

Your Answer _____

_____

Q–342

Why did the admission of Missouri in 1819 result in a controversy between the northern and southern members of Congress? How was this resolved?

Your Answer _____

_____

Correct Answers

A–340

They drafted a set of resolutions suggesting nullification and even secession if their interests were not protected against the growing influence of the South and the West.

A–341

Monroe was elected with only one electoral vote opposed.

A–342

Missouri's admission would upset the sectional balance in the Senate. As a compromise, Maine was admitted as a free state, Missouri was admitted as a slave state, and slavery was prohibited north of the 36°30′N latitude line in the Louisiana Territory.

Questions

Q–343

Why is the Jacksonian era known as the "age of the common man"?

Your Answer _____

_____

Q–344

How were the members of the Electoral College elected prior to 1824?

Your Answer _____

_____

Q–345

Why did John Quincy Adams win the election of 1824, and why did there appear to be a "corrupt bargain"?

Your Answer _____

_____

Correct Answers

A–343

Since most states had eliminated the property requirement for voting, the electorate was broadened to include almost all white males over twenty-one years of age.

A–344

By state legislatures

A–345

Since none of the candidates received a majority of electoral votes in 1824, the election went to the House of Representatives. Although Andrew Jackson had garnered the most electoral votes, Speaker of the House Henry Clay helped Adams win, after which time Adams appointed Clay as his secretary of state.

Questions

Q–346

John Quincy Adams's supporters called themselves
_____ _____.

Your Answer _____

Q–347

Why did John C. Calhoun anonymously publish the
South Carolina Exposition and Protest?

Your Answer _____

Q–348

What was the "Kitchen Cabinet"?

Your Answer _____

Correct Answers

A–346

National Republicans

A–347

He wanted to protest the tariff but protect his position as vice president.

A–348

The Kitchen Cabinet was a group of partisan supporters from whom President Andrew Jackson took counsel instead of relying on the advice of his appointed cabinet officers.

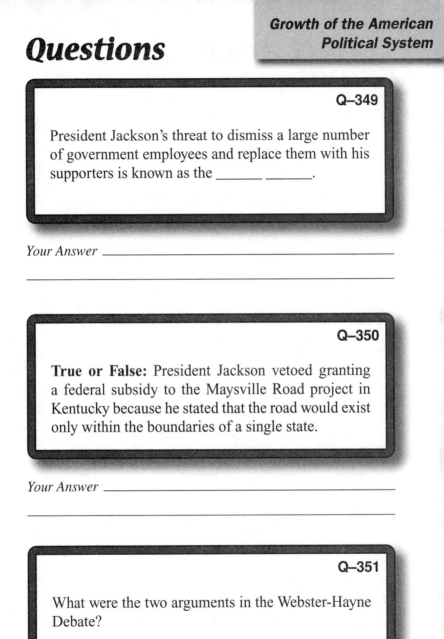

Q–349

President Jackson's threat to dismiss a large number of government employees and replace them with his supporters is known as the _____ _____.

Your Answer _____

Q–350

True or False: President Jackson vetoed granting a federal subsidy to the Maysville Road project in Kentucky because he stated that the road would exist only within the boundaries of a single state.

Your Answer _____

Q–351

What were the two arguments in the Webster-Hayne Debate?

Your Answer _____

Correct Answers

A–349

Spoils System

A–350

True

A–351

Senator Robert Hayne of South Carolina argued
against protective tariffs and referred to nullification as a solution. Senator Daniel Webster of
Massachusetts argued that the Union was indissol-
uble and that the federal government was sovereign
over the individual states.

Questions

Q–352

What was John C. Calhoun's reaction to the Tariff of 1832? What was President Jackson's response to Calhoun's position?

Your Answer _____

_____

Q–353

What did President Jackson's critics call him?

Your Answer _____

_____

Q–354

What was the major issue in the election of Andrew Jackson?

Your Answer _____

_____

Correct Answers

A–352

1) Calhoun resigned from the vice presidency and drew up the Ordinance of Nullification that ordered customs agents to stop collecting duties at Charleston Port.
2) Jackson obtained the Force Bill from Congress authorizing him to use federal troops to enforce the collection of taxes.

A–353

King Andrew

A–354

The rechartering of the National Bank

Questions

Q–355

The _____ _____ had emerged from the ruins of the National Republicans and other groups who opposed President Jackson's policies.

Your Answer _____

Q–356

Why did President Jackson, Henry Clay of Kentucky, and much of Congress not want to admit Texas into the Union when they first applied?

Your Answer _____

Q–357

In 1836, southern members of Congress pushed legislation through that forbade any discussion of slavery on the floor of Congress. What was it called?

Your Answer _____

Correct Answers

A–355

Whig Party

A–356

Texas's admittance would upset the sectional balance and stir up the slavery issue. Also, Mexico threatened war if the United States annexed Texas.

A–357

The Gag Rule

Q–358

What was the major issue that President Martin Van Buren had to deal with during his administration?

Your Answer _____

_____

Q–359

After President William Henry Harrison died, President John Tyler was sworn in to office. What was Tyler's relationship with the Whig leadership?

Your Answer _____

_____

Q–360

Who supported the Democratic and Whig parties during the Jacksonian era?

Your Answer _____

_____

Correct Answers

A–358

The financial chaos left by the death of the Second National Bank

A–359

Although Tyler ran as a Whig, he held many Democratic beliefs. As such, he vetoed much of the Whig legislation creating another Bank of the United States, raising tariffs, and completing internal improvements. He was then expelled from the Whig Party.

A–360

Working class, small merchants, and small farmers supported the Democrats. Northern businesses, manufacturing interests, and large southern planters supported the Whigs.

Q–361

What economic and foreign policies did President James Polk change during his presidency?

Your Answer _____

_____

Q–362

What was the Wilmot Proviso? What was its effect?

Your Answer _____

_____

Q–363

What were the three main parties in the 1848 election? How did each party stand on the issue of slavery in the territories?

Your Answer _____

_____

Correct Answers

A–361

1) Economic policies: Established a national treasury system, lowered tariffs
2) Foreign policies: Settled Oregon boundary dispute, acquired the Southwest and California

A–362

1) The Wilmot Proviso prohibited slavery in any territory that might be acquired from Mexico.
2) Although it was rejected in the Senate, it aroused emotions in southerners who felt it was unfair and northerners who argued the Mexican War was about extending slavery.

A–363

1) The three main parties were the Democrats, the Whigs, and the Free-Soilers.
2) The Democrats supported popular sovereignty. The Whigs ignored the issue. The Free-Soilers stood for keeping the territories free from slavery.

Questions

Q–364

What was the political result of the California gold rush of 1849?

Your Answer _____

Q–365

What three things did the Compromise of 1850 give the North?

Your Answer _____

Q–366

What three things did the Compromise of 1850 give the South?

Your Answer _____

Correct Answers

A–364

California's population soared from 14,000 to 100,000 in one year, and since there was no territorial government, California sought immediate admission as a state.

A–365

1) Admission of California as a free state
2) Abolition of the slave trade in the District of Columbia
3) Application of popular sovereignty in the Mexican cession outside of California

A–366

1) A tougher Fugitive Slave Law
2) Continuation of slavery in the District of Columbia
3) An agreement that Congress would have no jurisdiction over the interstate slave trade

Questions

Q–367

What were the main provisions of the Fugitive Slave Act of 1850? What was the northern response to it?

Your Answer _____

_____

Q–368

What was the immediate result of the Compromise of 1850?

Your Answer _____

_____

Q–369

What were two reasons why antislavery northerners were hostile toward President Franklin Pierce?

Your Answer _____

_____

Correct Answers

A–367

1) Alleged slaves in the North were denied a trial by jury, and U.S. citizens were required to help capture and return alleged fugitive slaves.
2) Several riots broke out in the North, and some states passed personal liberty laws in opposition.

A–368

The issue of slavery in the territories seemed to have been permanently settled and sectional harmony returned.

A–369

1) His administration appeared to be dominated by southerners, such as Secretary of War Jefferson Davis.
2) His actions, such as the Gadsden Purchase and the attempt to buy Cuba, seemed designed to favor the South.

Questions

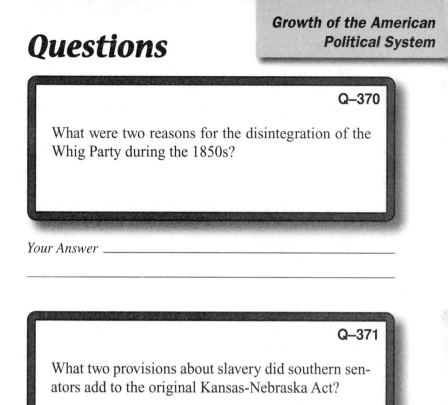

Q–370

What were two reasons for the disintegration of the Whig Party during the 1850s?

Your Answer _____

_____

Q–371

What two provisions about slavery did southern senators add to the original Kansas-Nebraska Act?

Your Answer _____

_____

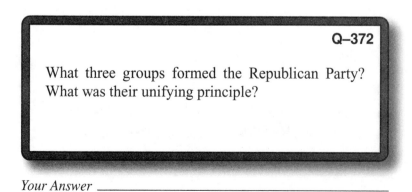

Q–372

What three groups formed the Republican Party? What was their unifying principle?

Your Answer _____

_____

Correct Answers

A–370

1) The issue of slavery, which divided the party along North-South lines
2) The nativist movement

A–371

The Missouri Compromise as it applied to Kansas and Nebraska was repealed, and the status of slavery in the two territories was to be decided by popular sovereignty.

A–372

1) Northern Democrats, former Whigs, and Know-Nothings
2) All three groups believed slavery should be banned from the territories.

Questions

Q–373

What was the reason for the election of a pro-slavery territorial government in Kansas? How did free-soil Kansans respond?

Your Answer _____

_____

Q–374

What did the South threaten to do if the Republicans won the 1856 presidential election?

Your Answer _____

_____

Q–375

What was the Lecompton Constitution?

Your Answer _____

_____

Correct Answers

A–373

1) A pro-slavery government was elected due to large-scale election fraud by "border ruffians" who entered Kansas from Missouri and voted often.
2) Free-soil Kansans denounced it and elected their own free-soil territorial government.

A–374

Southerners threatened to secede from the United States.

A–375

The Lecompton Constitution was a pro-slavery constitution for Kansas that was written by a fraudulent constitutional convention.

Q–376

What were the Lincoln-Douglas debates in 1858?

Your Answer _____

_____

Q–377

What was the "Freeport Doctrine"?

Your Answer _____

_____

Q–378

Who were the main presidential candidates and what were their parties in the election of 1860?

Your Answer _____

_____

Correct Answers

A–376

They were a series of seven debates held between Illinois Senator Stephen Douglas, who argued that popular sovereignty should dictate the slavery issue, and his electoral opponent Abraham Lincoln, who argued that slavery was a moral wrong.

A–377

The "Freeport Doctrine" was an argument by Senator Douglas in one of his debates with Abraham Lincoln. He argued that a territory could get around the *Dred Scott* decision by not passing the special laws that slave jurisdictions usually passed to support slavery.

A–378

1) Abraham Lincoln, Republican
2) Stephen Douglas, Northern Democrat
3) John Breckenridge, Southern Democrat
4) John Bell, Constitutional Union

Q–379

What was Senator John Crittenden's proposal to preserve the Union?

Your Answer _____

_____

Q–380

What bills did the U.S. government pass during the Civil War to economically assist western farmers?

Your Answer _____

_____

Q–381

Which of the four candidates in 1860 obtained a majority of the popular votes?

Your Answer _____

_____

Correct Answers

A–379

He proposed an extension of the Missouri Compromise line to the Pacific and prohibition of federal interference with slavery where it already existed. It was defeated due to President Lincoln's stance against the spread of slavery.

A–380

1) Homestead Act of 1862: Granted 160 acres to anyone who would farm it for five years
2) Morrill Land Grant Act of 1862: Offered large amounts of land to states to set up "agricultural and mechanical" colleges

A–381

None of the four candidates obtained a majority of the popular votes.

Questions

Q–382

What was the National Union Party?

Your Answer _____

_____

Q–383

What effect did the capture of Atlanta have on the election of 1864?

Your Answer _____

_____

Q–384

What was the Wade-Davis Bill?

Your Answer _____

_____

Correct Answers

A–382

A combination of the Republican Party with loyal or "War" Democrats

A–383

The capture of Atlanta by Union troops provided a morale boost to the North and ensured the reelection of President Lincoln. Prior to the fall of Atlanta, many people were looking to the Democrats to negotiate a peace with the South.

A–384

The Wade-Davis Bill stated that a loyal state government could be established if a majority of voters swore they had never been disloyal to the Union. President Lincoln "pocket vetoed" the bill.

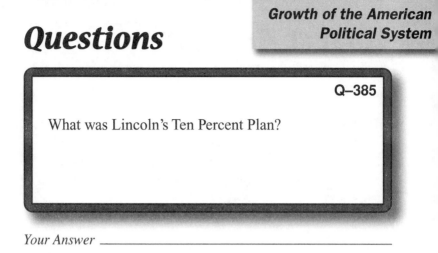

Q–385

What was Lincoln's Ten Percent Plan?

Your Answer _____

_____

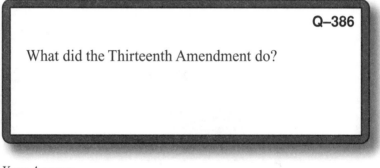

Q–386

What did the Thirteenth Amendment do?

Your Answer _____

_____

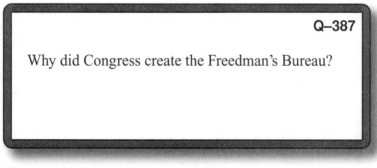

Q–387

Why did Congress create the Freedman's Bureau?

Your Answer _____

_____

Correct Answers

A–385

The Ten Percent Plan said that as soon as 10 percent of the voters of a state had taken a loyalty oath to the Union and agreed to the abolition of slavery, a loyal state government could be formed.

A–386

The Thirteenth Amendment abolished slavery.

A–387

To provide food, clothing, and education, and generally look after the interests of former slaves

Questions

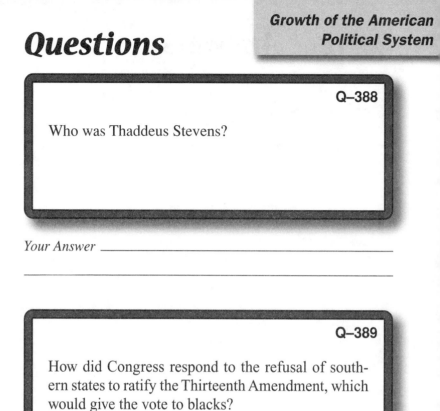

Q–388

Who was Thaddeus Stevens?

Your Answer _____

_____

Q–389

How did Congress respond to the refusal of southern states to ratify the Thirteenth Amendment, which would give the vote to blacks?

Your Answer _____

_____

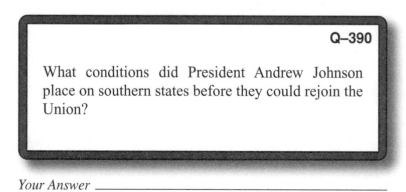

Q–390

What conditions did President Andrew Johnson place on southern states before they could rejoin the Union?

Your Answer _____

_____

Correct Answers

A–388

He was a Radical Republican member of Congress.

A–389

Congress passed a Civil Rights Act and extended the powers of the Freedman's Bureau.

A–390

He required them to ratify the Thirteenth Amendment, repudiate Confederate debts, renounce secession, and give the vote to blacks.

Questions

Q–391

What was the Military Reconstruction Act of 1866?

Your Answer _____

_____

Q–392

What was the Tenure of Office Act?

Your Answer _____

_____

Q–393

How did Congress respond when President Andrew Johnson fired his secretary of war, Edwin M. Stanton, from his cabinet?

Your Answer _____

_____

Correct Answers

A–391

The Military Reconstruction Act of 1866 divided the South into five military districts to be ruled by military governors.

A–392

The Tenure of Office Act established that federal officials whose appointment required Senate approval could not be removed from office without the Senate's consent. Congress passed the law in order to prevent President Andrew Johnson from dismissing any of his cabinet members, specifically Secretary of War Edwin M. Stanton.

A–393

The House of Representatives impeached Johnson, and the Senate came within one vote of removing him from office.

Questions

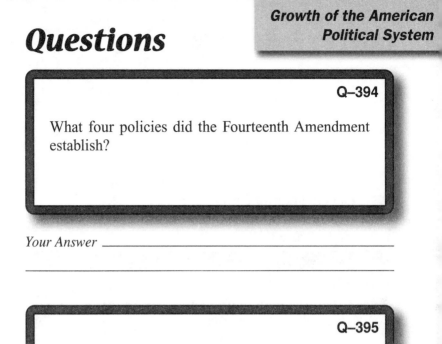

Q–394

What four policies did the Fourteenth Amendment establish?

Your Answer _____

_____

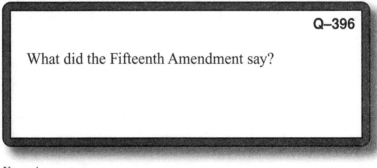

Q–395

How did the vote of 700,000 blacks, in the southern states under military rule, affect the 1868 election?

Your Answer _____

_____

Q–396

What did the Fifteenth Amendment say?

Your Answer _____

_____

Correct Answers

A–394

1) The Fourteenth Amendment forbade states to deny various rights to citizens.
2) It forbade the paying of the Confederate debt.
3) It denied Congressional representation to states that did not give blacks the right to vote.
4) It made former Confederates ineligible to hold public office.

A–395

The black vote probably gave the election to Ulysses S. Grant.

A–396

The Fifteenth Amendment gave blacks the right to vote.

Questions

Q–397

Why did southern states vote to ratify the Fifteenth Amendment?

Your Answer _____

_____

Q–398

Who was William Marcy Tweed?

Your Answer _____

_____

Q–399

What scandals erupted during President Grant's administration? Why was it so corrupt?

Your Answer _____

_____

Correct Answers

A–397

They had no choice if they were to be readmitted to the Union.

A–398

William Marcy Tweed was head of the Tammany Hall political machine in New York City.

A–399

1) The Gould-Fisk gold scandal; Credit Mobilier scandal; Whiskey Ring; Belknap accepting bribes
2) Although Grant was an honest man, he was loyal and trusted dishonest people.

Questions

Q–400

Who were the Liberal Republicans?

Your Answer _____

Q–401

What was the tactic known as "waving the bloody shirt"?

Your Answer _____

Q–402

What was the Compromise of 1877?

Your Answer _____

Correct Answers

A–400

The Liberal Republicans were a faction of the Republican Party that opposed corruption and favored sectional harmony, hard money, and a laissez-faire approach to economics.

A–401

It was a tactic in which Republicans urged northerners to vote the way they had shot during the Civil War. It suggested that a Democratic victory would be the same as a Confederate victory.

A–402

The Compromise of 1877 was an agreement under which Rutherford B. Hayes promised to show consideration for southern interests, end Reconstruction, and withdraw the remaining federal troops from the South in exchange for the Democrats going along with his election to the presidency.

Questions

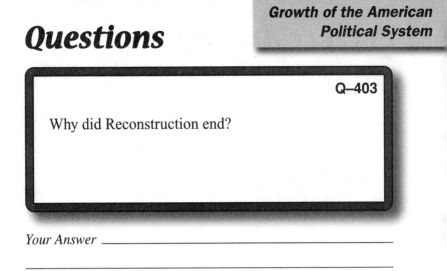

Q–403

Why did Reconstruction end?

Your Answer _____

_____

Q–404

What were "Jim Crow" laws?

Your Answer _____

_____

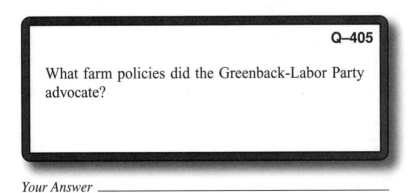

Q–405

What farm policies did the Greenback-Labor Party advocate?

Your Answer _____

_____

Correct Answers

A–403

The North lost interest as a result of government corruption, a depression, general weariness about the difficulty of remaking southern society, and the death of Radical Reconstruction leaders.

A–404

They were laws that separated the races.

A–405

1) Inflated farm prices
2) The cooperative marketing of produce

Questions

Q–406

In which direction did the balance of power tip during the Gilded Age, toward a strong president or a strong Congress?

Your Answer _____

_____

Q–407

Who were the "Stalwarts" and the "Half-Breeds"?

Your Answer _____

_____

Q–408

What happened to James A. Garfield soon after his election as president?

Your Answer _____

_____

Correct Answers

A–406

A strong Congress

A–407

1) The "Stalwarts" favored the old spoils system of political patronage.
2) The "Half-breeds" favored civil service reform and merit appointments to government positions.

A–408

A disappointed patronage seeker named Charles Guiteau assassinated him.

Questions

Q–409

What was the Pendleton Act of 1883?

Your Answer _____

_____

Q–410

Who were the "Mugwumps"? How did they affect the election of 1884?

Your Answer _____

_____

Q–411

Who was the only Democrat elected president in the half century after the Civil War?

Your Answer _____

_____

Correct Answers

The Pendleton Act of 1883 set up open-competitive examinations for civil service positions.

1) The "Mugwumps" were independent Republicans who favored more civil service reform.
2) They deserted the Republican candidate. This led to the election of Democrat Grover Cleveland.

Grover Cleveland

Questions

Q–412

What did the Interstate Commerce Act of 1887 create?

Your Answer _____

Q–413

How did the Dependent Pensions Act of 1890 change public policy regarding army veterans?

Your Answer _____

Q–414

What policies did the Populist Party advocate?

Your Answer _____

Correct Answers

A–412

The Interstate Commerce Act of 1887 set up a commission to oversee fair railway rates, prohibit rebates, end discriminatory practices, and require annual financial reports from railroads.

A–413

The Dependent Pensions Act of 1890 provided pensions to army veterans and their dependents for the first time.

A–414

1) Coinage of silver at the ratio of 16 to 1
2) An eight-hour workday
3) The abolition of private armies used to break strikes
4) Direct election of senators
5) The right of initiative and referendum
6) The secret ballot
7) A graduated income tax

Questions

Q–415

Who was William Jennings Bryan?

Your Answer _____

_____

Q–416

What was the "Cross of Gold" speech?

Your Answer _____

_____

Q–417

How did Theodore Roosevelt become president?

Your Answer _____

_____

Correct Answers

A–415

William Jennings Bryan was the three-time Democratic nominee for president. He delivered the "Cross of Gold" speech advocating "free silver." He advocated for government regulation of industries and lower tariffs. He also ran as an anti-imperialist and led the prosecution in the Scopes Monkey Trial.

A–416

A speech delivered in 1896 by William Jennings Bryan in support of the coinage of silver

A–417

He was vice president when President William McKinley was assassinated.

Q–418

What was the "square deal"?

Your Answer _____

_____

Q–419

What was President Theodore Roosevelt's attitude toward trusts?

Your Answer _____

_____

Q–420

What powers did the Hepburn Act of 1906 give to the Interstate Commerce Commission (ICC)?

Your Answer _____

_____

Correct Answers

A–418

A policy followed by President Theodore Roosevelt to restrain corporate monopoly and promote economic competition

A–419

He believed that illegal monopolies should be broken up and that the federal government should regulate large corporations for the good of the public.

A–420

The Hepburn Act gave the ICC the power to set fair freight rates; regulate pipelines, bridges, and express companies; and set up a uniform system of accounting for transportation companies.

Questions

Q–421

What were the terms of the Pure Food and Drug Act of 1906?

Your Answer _____

_____

Q–422

What two monopolies did President Theodore Roosevelt's administration bring suit against?

Your Answer _____

_____

Q–423

Who was the presidential candidate of the Socialists in 1908?

Your Answer _____

_____

Correct Answers

A–421

The act prohibited the manufacture, sale, and transportation of foods and drugs that were adulterated or fraudulently labeled.

A–422

The Northern Securities Company (railroads) and the Standard Oil Company (oil)

A–423

Eugene Debs

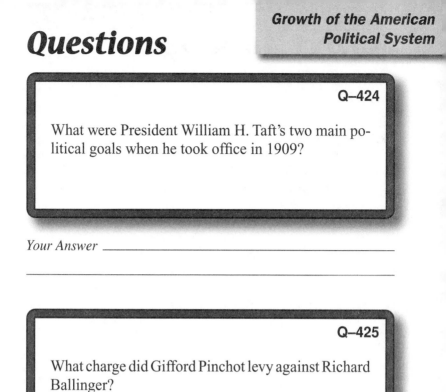

Q–424

What were President William H. Taft's two main political goals when he took office in 1909?

Your Answer _____

_____

Q–425

What charge did Gifford Pinchot levy against Richard Ballinger?

Your Answer _____

_____

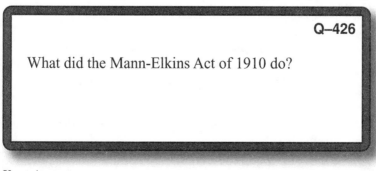

Q–426

What did the Mann-Elkins Act of 1910 do?

Your Answer _____

_____

Correct Answers

A–424

Taft wanted to continue President Theodore Roosevelt's trust-busting policies and hoped to reconcile the Republican Party's old guard conservatives and its young progressive reformers.

A–425

Pinchot accused Ballinger of giving away the nation's natural resources to private corporate interests.

A–426

1) The Mann-Elkins Act gave the Interstate Commerce Commission (ICC) regulatory powers over cable and wireless companies and telephone and telegraph lines.
2) It gave the ICC power to suspend questionable rates.
3) It set up a commerce court to handle rate dispute cases.

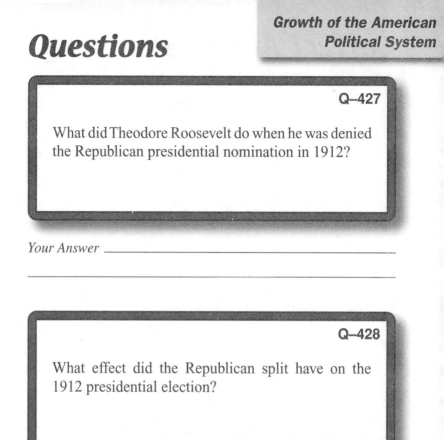

Q–427

What did Theodore Roosevelt do when he was denied the Republican presidential nomination in 1912?

Your Answer _____

_____

Q–428

What effect did the Republican split have on the 1912 presidential election?

Your Answer _____

_____

Q–429

How did Theodore Roosevelt and Woodrow Wilson differ in their attitudes toward big business?

Your Answer _____

_____

Correct Answers

He formed the Progressive, or Bull Moose, Party.

The split paved the way for a Democratic victory.

1) Roosevelt favored regulation of big business.
2) Wilson favored breaking up large corporations.

Questions

Q–430

What did the Sixteenth Amendment to the Constitution provide?

Your Answer _____

Q–431

What did the Seventeenth Amendment provide for?

Your Answer _____

Q–432

What was the purpose of the Federal Trade Commission?

Your Answer _____

Correct Answers

A–430

The amendment provided for a graduated income tax.

A–431

The Seventeenth Amendment provided for the direct election of U.S. senators.

A–432

To investigate unfair business practices

Questions

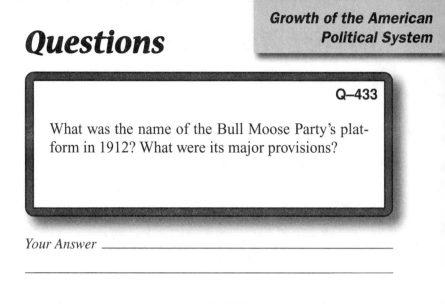

Q–433

What was the name of the Bull Moose Party's platform in 1912? What were its major provisions?

Your Answer _____

_____

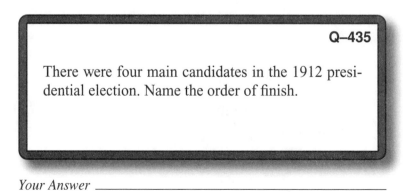

Q–434

In the election of 1912, what was the term used to describe Democratic nominee Woodrow Wilson's platform? What were two features of this platform?

Your Answer _____

_____

Q–435

There were four main candidates in the 1912 presidential election. Name the order of finish.

Your Answer _____

_____

Correct Answers

A–433

1) The New Nationalism
2) Federal old age; unemployment; accident insurance; eight-hour workdays; women's suffrage; abolition of child labor; and expanded public health services

A–434

1) Wilson's platform was called the New Freedom.
2) Two features of the platform were to restore economic competition through the breakup of monopolies and to lower tariffs.

A–435

1) Woodrow Wilson
2) Theodore Roosevelt
3) William Howard Taft
4) Eugene Debs

Q–436

What were the three main features of President Woodrow Wilson's legislative promise in 1913?

Your Answer _____

_____

Q–437

What was the consequence of the 1918 congressional elections on President Wilson's international stature?

Your Answer _____

_____

Q–438

What did the Nineteenth Amendment provide for and when did Congress approve it?

Your Answer _____

_____

Correct Answers

A–436

1) Reduction of the tariff
2) Return of the banking and currency laws
3) Improvements in the antitrust laws

A–437

Wilson had appealed to the voters to elect a Democratic Congress, saying to do otherwise would be a repudiation of his leadership in European affairs. The voters gave the Republicans a slim margin in both houses in the election. This undermined Wilson's political support at home and his stature in the eyes of world leaders.

A–438

The Nineteenth Amendment provided for woman suffrage, and Congress approved it in 1919.

Questions

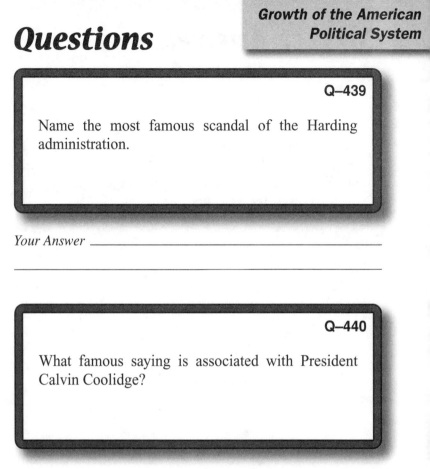

Q–439

Name the most famous scandal of the Harding administration.

Your Answer _____

_____

Q–440

What famous saying is associated with President Calvin Coolidge?

Your Answer _____

_____

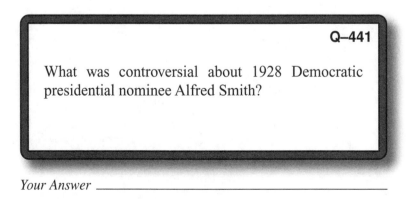

Q–441

What was controversial about 1928 Democratic presidential nominee Alfred Smith?

Your Answer _____

_____

Correct Answers

A–439

The most famous scandal of the Harding administration was the Teapot Dome Scandal. Secretary of the Interior Albert B. Fall was convicted, fined, and imprisoned for accepting bribes in exchange for leasing oil reserves at Teapot Dome, Wyoming.

A–440

"The business of the United States is business."

A–441

He was Catholic and against Prohibition.

Questions

Q–442

What was the Garner-Wagner Bill? Why did President Herbert Hoover veto it?

Your Answer _____

_____

Q–443

What was President Franklin D. Roosevelt's inner circle of unofficial advisers called?

Your Answer _____

_____

Q–444

Who was the first woman appointed to a cabinet position?

Your Answer _____

_____

Correct Answers

A–442

1) The Garner-Wagner Bill would have appropriated federal funds for relief of the needy.
2) Hoover vetoed the bill because he was philosophically opposed to using federal funds for that purpose.

A–443

The Brain Trust

A–444

Frances Perkins was appointed secretary of labor by President Franklin Roosevelt in 1933.

Questions

Q–445

What was the objective of the Agricultural Adjustment Act of 1933?

Your Answer _____

_____

Q–446

What was the Twenty-first Amendment to the Constitution? When did it take effect?

Your Answer _____

_____

Q–447

What memorable slogan did President Franklin Roosevelt use in his inaugural speech on March 4, 1933?

Your Answer _____

_____

Correct Answers

A–445

The act sought to return farm prices to parity with those of the 1909 to 1914 period.

A–446

1) The Twenty-first Amendment repealed Prohibition.
2) It took effect in December 1933.

A–447

"The only thing we have to fear is fear itself."

Questions

Q–448

What was the term used to describe the legislation passed between 1933 and 1935?

Your Answer _____

_____

Q–449

Why was the Federal Housing Administration (FHA) created?

Your Answer _____

_____

Q–450

What was the Federal Emergency Relief Act? How was it administered?

Your Answer _____

_____

Correct Answers

A–448

The First New Deal

A–449

The FHA was created to insure long-term, low-interest mortgages for home construction and repair.

A–450

1) This law, passed in the first one hundred days of the Roosevelt administration, appropriated $500 million for aid to the poor to be distributed by state and local governments.
2) It was administered by the Federal Emergency Relief Administration.

Questions

Q–451

How did the Public Works Administration work? What was its objective?

Your Answer _____

Q–452

What were three common conservative criticisms of the First New Deal?

Your Answer _____

Q–453

Describe the composition of the New Deal coalition.

Your Answer _____

Correct Answers

A–451

1) Federal money was distributed to state and local governments for building projects such as schools, highways, and hospitals.
2) The objective was to "prime the pump" of the economy by creating construction jobs.

A–452

1) Deficit financing
2) Federal spending for relief
3) Government regulation of business

A–453

1) Solid South
2) Ethnic groups in big cities
3) Midwestern farmers
4) Union workers
5) Blacks

Q–454

What prompted President Franklin Roosevelt's ill-fated "court packing" proposal?

Your Answer _____

Q–455

When was the Wagner-Steagall Act passed? What did it do?

Your Answer _____

Q–456

Explain the Second Agricultural Adjustment Act of February 1938.

Your Answer _____

Correct Answers

A–454

He was frustrated over the refusal of older, conservative judges to retire.

A–455

1) 1937
2) It established the United States Housing Authority (USHA), which could borrow money to lend to local agencies.

A–456

This act appropriated funds for soil-conservation payments to farmers who would remove land from production.

Questions

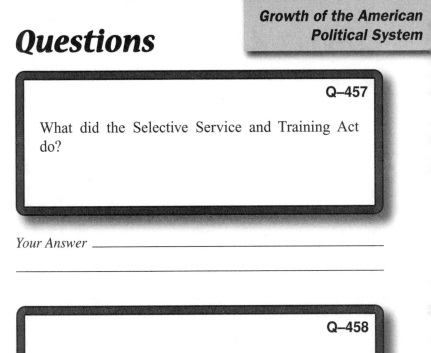

Q–457

What did the Selective Service and Training Act do?

Your Answer _____

_____

Q–458

What was significant about the Democrats nominating President Franklin Roosevelt for re-election in 1940?

Your Answer _____

_____

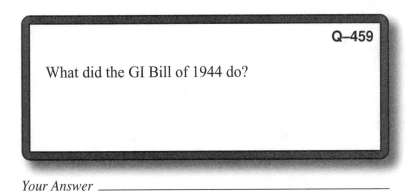

Q–459

What did the GI Bill of 1944 do?

Your Answer _____

_____

Correct Answers

A–457

Approved in September of 1940, the act created the nation's first peacetime draft.

A–458

Since Roosevelt was being nominated for a third term, it broke with a tradition that had existed since the time of Washington that presidents would only serve two terms.

A–459

The GI Bill provided returning servicemen with $13 billion in aid ranging from education to housing.

Questions

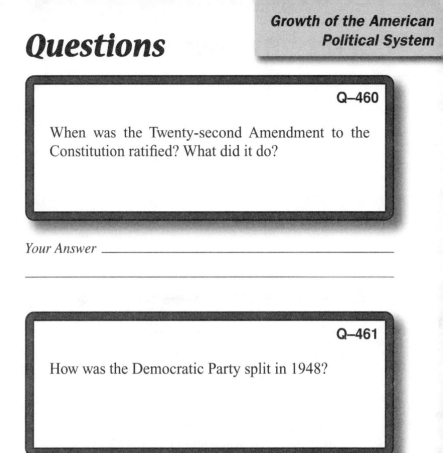

Q–460

When was the Twenty-second Amendment to the Constitution ratified? What did it do?

Your Answer _____

_____

Q–461

How was the Democratic Party split in 1948?

Your Answer _____

_____

Q–462

What was the Fair Deal Program?

Your Answer _____

_____

Correct Answers

A–460

1) 1951
2) The amendment limited the president to two terms.

A–461

1) Many southern Democrats, angered by President Harry Truman's support of civil rights, split off to form the Dixiecrat Party headed by South Carolina Governor Strom Thurmond.
2) The Progressive Party was formed as a protest against the Cold War policies of the Truman administration. It nominated former Vice President Henry Wallace for president.

A–462

The Fair Deal Program was President Truman's proposals to enlarge and extend the New Deal. Some of its provisions included increasing the minimum wage, extending Social Security, and building more public housing.

Questions

Q–463

What was the purpose of the Loyalty Review Board? Why was it created?

Your Answer _____

_____

Q–464

What speech propelled Senator Joseph McCarthy of Wisconsin into national prominence?

Your Answer _____

_____

Q–465

What were the results of the 1952 presidential election? What was especially significant about the election?

Your Answer _____

_____

Correct Answers

A–463

1) The Loyalty Review Board's purpose was to review the patriotism and loyalty of government employees.
2) It was created in response to criticism that the Truman administration was soft on Communism.

A–464

During a February 9, 1950, speech, McCarthy stated that he had a list of known Communists who were working in the State Department.

A–465

1) Republican Dwight Eisenhower defeated Democrat Adlai Stevenson.
2) For the first time since Reconstruction, the Republicans won some southern states.

Questions

Q–466

How did President Eisenhower describe his legislative program?

Your Answer _____

_____

Q–467

How did John F. Kennedy defuse the issue of his Catholicism during the 1960 campaign?

Your Answer _____

_____

Q–468

What were generally considered the pivotal events of the 1960 presidential election?

Your Answer _____

_____

Correct Answers

A–466

"Dynamic Conservatism"

A–467

He told a gathering of Protestant ministers that he accepted separation of church and state and that Catholic leaders would not tell him how to act as president.

A–468

A series of televised debates between John F. Kennedy and Richard Nixon that helped create a positive image for Kennedy.

Q–469

What was the aim of the Economic Opportunity Act of 1964?

Your Answer _____

_____

Q–470

What was the Medicare Act of 1965?

Your Answer _____

_____

Q–471

What was the major issue in Eugene McCarthy's 1968 presidential campaign? What was the significance of McCarthy's performance in the New Hampshire primary?

Your Answer _____

_____

Correct Answers

A–469

The act sought to eliminate poverty by establishing a Job Corps, community action programs, educational programs, work-study programs, job training, loans for small businesses, and VISTA, "a domestic peace corps."

A–470

The act combined hospital insurance for retired people with a voluntary plan to cover physician bills.

A–471

1) Opposition to the Vietnam War
2) McCarthy's surprisingly strong second place showing contributed to President Lyndon Johnson's withdrawal from the race.

Q–472

What explains the appeal of Governor George Wallace in the 1968 presidential election?

Your Answer _____

_____

Q–473

What was President Richard Nixon's New Federalism?

Your Answer _____

_____

Q–474

When was the voting age lowered to 18?

Your Answer _____

_____

Correct Answers

A–472

Fears generated by protestors, black militants, and an expanding bureaucracy

A–473

New Federalism was a revenue-sharing plan, passed in 1972, to distribute $30 billion of federal revenue to the states.

A–474

1970

Questions

Q–475

When was the Watergate break-in? What happened at the break-in?

Your Answer _____

_____

Q–476

Why did Vice President Spiro Agnew resign in October of 1973?

Your Answer _____

_____

Q–477

What three articles of impeachment against President Nixon did the House Judiciary Committee adopt?

Your Answer _____

_____

Correct Answers

A–475

1) June 17, 1972
2) Four men associated with President Nixon's re-election campaign broke into Democratic head-quarters and the Watergate apartment complex. They were caught going through files and install-ing eavesdropping devices.

A–476

He was accused of income-tax fraud and of accept-ing bribes while a local official in Maryland.

A–477

The committee charged the president with obstruct-ing justice, misusing presidential power, and failing to obey its subpoenas.

Questions

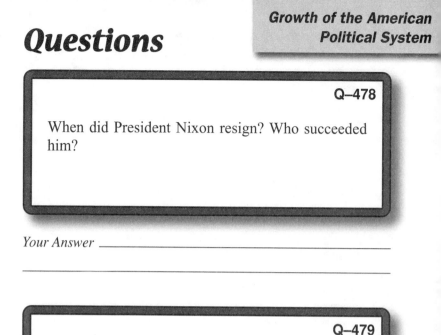

Q–478

When did President Nixon resign? Who succeeded him?

Your Answer _____

_____

Q–479

What did the War Powers Act of 1973 accomplish?

Your Answer _____

_____

Q–480

What did the Freedom of Information Act do?

Your Answer _____

_____

Correct Answers

A–478

1) August 8, 1974
2) Vice President Gerald Ford

A–479

The act required congressional approval of any commitment of combat troops beyond ninety days.

A–480

The Freedom of Information Act required the government to act promptly when asked for information and to prove its case for classification when attempting to withhold information on grounds of national security.

Questions

Q–481

Which president offered amnesty to Americans who had fled the draft and gone to other countries during the Vietnam War?

Your Answer _____

_____

Q–482

What senior citizen lobbying group became influential during the 1980s?

Your Answer _____

_____

Q–483

What happened to the proposed Equal Rights Amendment?

Your Answer _____

_____

Correct Answers

A–481

President Jimmy Carter

A–482

American Association of Retired Persons (AARP)

A–483

The Equal Rights Amendment was approved by Congress in 1972 but was never ratified by the required thirty-eight states.

Questions

Q–484

What were the positions of the "Moral Majority" political movement?

Your Answer _____

_____

Q–485

What was George H. W. Bush's famous "pledge" during the 1988 campaign?

Your Answer _____

_____

Q–486

What was the 1990 Americans with Disabilities Act?

Your Answer _____

_____

Correct Answers

A–484

Members of the Moral Majority favored prayer in school, opposed abortion and the Equal Rights Amendment, and supported a strong national defense.

A–485

"No new taxes"

A–486

A law barring discrimination against people with physical or mental disabilities

Questions

Q–487

What was significant about Ross Perot's performance during the 1992 presidential election?

Your Answer _____

_____

Q–488

What were the main components of the Clinton administration's health care reform plan? Who were the plan's major opponents?

Your Answer _____

_____

Q–489

What was the first controversy of the Clinton administration?

Your Answer _____

_____

Correct Answers

A–487

Perot won 19 percent of the popular vote, which was the best performance by a candidate not nominated by the two major parties since Theodore Roosevelt in 1912.

A–488

1) Universal coverage with a guaranteed benefits package and managed competition through health care alliances that would bargain with insurance companies
2) Republicans, small businesses, and insurance and medical-business interests

A–489

President Bill Clinton proposed to lift the ban on gays and lesbians in the military.

STOP **Take Test-Readiness Quiz 2 on CD**
(to review questions 238-489)

Q–490

What was the Whitewater scandal?

Your Answer _____

_____

Q–491

What was the significance of the 1994 Congressional elections?

Your Answer _____

_____

Economic Trends

Q–492

What were *encomiendas*?

Your Answer _____

_____

Correct Answers

A–490

President Clinton was criticized for wrongdoings in the Whitewater real estate developments in which he had been an investor, while governor of Arkansas. His partner was James B. McDougal, owner of a failed savings and loan institution.

A–491

They gave Republicans control of both houses of Congress for the first time since 1952.

A–492

Encomiendas were large manors or estates with Indian slaves. They were developed to reward successful conquistadores and help the conquistadors deal with labor shortages.

Q–493

What lucrative trade was opened by the French and the Indians?

Your Answer ⎯⎯⎯⎯⎯⎯⎯⎯⎯⎯⎯⎯⎯⎯⎯⎯⎯⎯⎯⎯⎯⎯

⎯⎯⎯⎯⎯⎯⎯⎯⎯⎯⎯⎯⎯⎯⎯⎯⎯⎯⎯⎯⎯⎯⎯⎯⎯⎯⎯⎯

Q–494

What was the economic base of the northern colonies?

Your Answer ⎯⎯⎯⎯⎯⎯⎯⎯⎯⎯⎯⎯⎯⎯⎯⎯⎯⎯⎯⎯⎯⎯

⎯⎯⎯⎯⎯⎯⎯⎯⎯⎯⎯⎯⎯⎯⎯⎯⎯⎯⎯⎯⎯⎯⎯⎯⎯⎯⎯⎯

Q–495

What was the economic base of the southern colonies?

Your Answer ⎯⎯⎯⎯⎯⎯⎯⎯⎯⎯⎯⎯⎯⎯⎯⎯⎯⎯⎯⎯⎯⎯

⎯⎯⎯⎯⎯⎯⎯⎯⎯⎯⎯⎯⎯⎯⎯⎯⎯⎯⎯⎯⎯⎯⎯⎯⎯⎯⎯⎯

Correct Answers

A–493

The fur trade

A–494

1) New England: Shipping, shipbuilding, fishing, small farming
2) Middle Colonies: Farming (aka the "bread basket"), shipping

---

A–495

1) Chesapeake Bay (Maryland, Virginia): Tobacco
2) North Carolina: Tobacco
3) South Carolina: Rice and indigo

Questions

Q–496

True or False: After 1650, British authorities believed that the American colonists should have unregulated trade restrictions.

Your Answer _____

Q–497

Which American colonies prospered from England's mercantilistic policy?

Your Answer _____

Q–498

What three economic proposals did Alexander Hamilton endorse in *The Report on Public Credit* to handle the economic crisis faced by the government of the United States?

Your Answer _____

Correct Answers

A–496

False. British authorities believed that American trade should be regulated for the benefit of the mother country.

A–497

New England—it encouraged large-scale shipbuilding.

A–498

1) Funding of the national debt at face value
2) Federal assumption of the states' debt
3) The establishment of a national bank

Questions

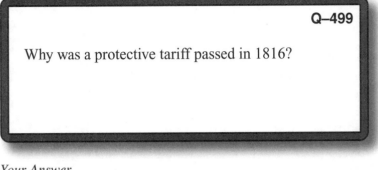

Q–499

Why was a protective tariff passed in 1816?

Your Answer _____

_____

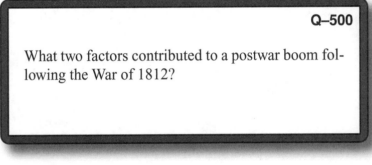

Q–500

What two factors contributed to a postwar boom following the War of 1812?

Your Answer _____

_____

Q–501

What major factors led to the Depression of 1819?

Your Answer _____

_____

Correct Answers

A–499

To slow the flood of cheap British manufactures in the United States

A–500

High foreign demand for American cotton, tobacco, and grain, and the Second National Bank's overly liberal credit policies

A–501

A major influx of British goods at cut-rate prices hurt American manufacturers.

Q–502

List two reasons why the West was most severely hit by the Depression of 1819.

Your Answer _____

Q–503

What were the main industries in the Northeast?

Your Answer _____

Q–504

In 1830, which city was America's largest city and primary trade center?

Your Answer _____

Correct Answers

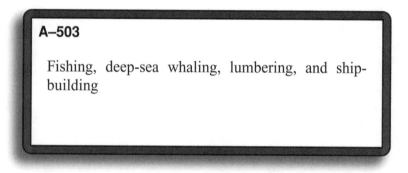

A–502

1) Economic dependency
2) Heavy speculation in western lands

A–503

Fishing, deep-sea whaling, lumbering, and ship-building

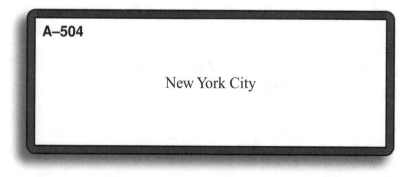

A–504

New York City

Questions

Q–505

In what industry did the factory system in the United States start?

Your Answer _____

_____

Q–506

What was the Lowell System?

Your Answer _____

_____

Q–507

Why was the "rotating labor supply" of the Lowell System ideal for factory owners?

Your Answer _____

_____

Correct Answers

A–505

The textile industry

A–506

The Lowell System (first developed in Lowell, Massachusetts) was a popular way to staff New England factories. Young farm women were recruited to work in the factories in mill towns and were provided dormitory housing as part of their employment. They worked for short periods of time before getting married.

A–507

The factory owners paid girls low wages and offered poor working conditions. However, since these girls only worked a short time, they did not agitate for better wages or conditions.

Q–508

Why were skilled artisans less important in the factories?

Your Answer _____

_____

Q–509

Why was the new tariff bill of 1828 known as the "Tariff of Abominations" by Southern planters?

Your Answer _____

_____

Q–510

During the Jacksonian era, why did northeasterners oppose the government's disposal of lands at cheap prices?

Your Answer _____

_____

Correct Answers

A–508

Repetitive processes could be performed by relatively unskilled workers.

A–509

The finished bill included higher import duties for many goods that were bought by Southern planters.

A–510

The policy would lure away their labor supply and drive up wages.

Questions

Q–511

Why did President Andrew Jackson issue the Specie Circular?

Your Answer _____

_____

Q–512

What did President Jackson do to destroy the Bank of the United States?

Your Answer _____

_____

Q–513

What professional occupation was dominated by women in the 1830s and 1840s?

Your Answer _____

_____

Correct Answers

A–511

He wanted to slow down the inflationary spiral, and this required that public land be paid for in hard money, not paper money or credit.

A–512

Jackson removed federal deposits from the Bank of the United States and redistributed the money into his "pet banks" (various state and local banks).

A–513

School teaching

Q–514

By 1850, over one-half of the manufacturing plants established were located in the _____ states.

Your Answer _____

_____

Q–515

What product replaced water as a major source of industrial power?

Your Answer _____

_____

Q–516

Which new industry was the largest consumer of iron in the nineteenth century?

Your Answer _____

_____

Correct Answers

A–514

northeastern

A–515

Coal

A–516

The railroad industry

Q–517

Why did the influx of immigrants weaken the bargaining position of the early labor union?

Your Answer _____

_____

Q–518

In the second quarter of the nineteenth century, the South had an _____ economy.

Your Answer _____

_____

Q–519

Prior to the Civil War, what was the occupation of most southern whites?

Your Answer _____

_____

Correct Answers

A–517

Immigrants were willing to work for low wages and provided an available labor supply.

A–518

agrarian

A–519

They were yeoman farmers who mostly grew corn.

Q–520

When the Civil War broke out in 1861, what percent of the factories lay in the North?

Your Answer _____

_____

Q–521

List three main manufacturing industries in the South during the 1820s and 1830s.

Your Answer _____

_____

Q–522

Why were southerners so wedded to the plantation system?

Your Answer _____

_____

Correct Answers

A–520

81 percent

A–521

1) Textiles
2) Iron production
3) Flour milling

A–522

Cotton was profitable, and planters had most of their money invested in land and slaves. Planters did not have the capital to invest in manufacturing or commerce.

Questions

Q–523

Why did a southern legislator remark "Cotton is King"?

Your Answer _____

_____

Q–524

What were the three basic causes of the Panic of 1857?

Your Answer _____

_____

Q–525

How did the North and South interpret the Panic of 1857?

Your Answer _____

_____

Correct Answers

A–523

By 1860, cotton accounted for two-thirds of the value of U.S. exports.

A–524

1) Overspeculation in railroads and land
2) Faulty banking practices
3) An interruption in the flow of European capital into the United States because of the Crimean War

A–525

The North blamed it on low tariffs. However, the South believed it showed the strength of "King Cotton" and the superiority of the southern slave system. It gave the South the sense that they did not need the North.

Questions

Q–526

What new tax did the North impose in order to help finance the Civil War?

Your Answer _____

_____

Q–527

What are "greenbacks"? Why do creditors/business-men dislike them, and why do debtors favor them?

Your Answer _____

_____

Q–528

Why did many farmers go into debt during the Civil War?

Your Answer _____

_____

Correct Answers

A–526

The income tax

A–527

1) A currency not backed by specie first issued in 1862.
2) Creditors/businessmen dislike them and debtors favor them because "greenbacks" cause inflation, which decreases the value of the money. So, debtors can pay off debt in money that is less valuable than the gold they borrowed.

A–528

They overexpanded their operations by buying more land and machinery than they could afford.

Q–529

What was the Gilded Age?

Your Answer _____

_____

Q–530

Who were the robber barons?

Your Answer _____

_____

Q–531

About how much of the country's wealth was controlled by the top 10 percent of the American population in the period after the Civil War?

Your Answer _____

_____

Correct Answers

The period between the 1870s and 1890s in America

Powerful, often ruthless, capitalists who owed their wealth to exploitative business practices

About 90 percent

Questions

Q–532

Who helped develop the modern steel industry in the United States?

Your Answer _____

_____

Q–533

Who founded the Standard Oil Company and helped develop the modern oil industry in the United States?

Your Answer _____

_____

Q–534

Who was Gustavus Swift?

Your Answer _____

_____

Correct Answers

A–532

Andrew Carnegie

A–533

John D. Rockefeller

A–534

Gustavus Swift was a leader in the meat-processing
industry in the 1880s.

Questions

Q–535

Who was J. P. Morgan?

Your Answer _____

_____

Q–536

What two national labor organizations were formed during the 1860s?

Your Answer _____

_____

Q–537

What led to the Panic of 1873?

Your Answer _____

_____

Correct Answers

A–535

J. P. Morgan was a leader in the banking industry in the 1880s.

A–536

The National Labor Union and the Knights of Labor

A–537

The overexpansion of railroads, an economic downturn in Europe, and the failure of the American financial firm of Jay Cooke

Questions

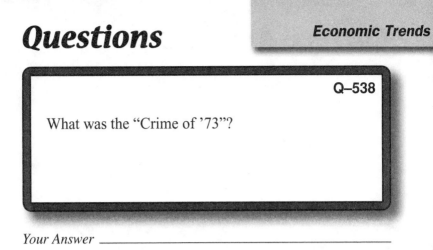

Q–538

What was the "Crime of '73"?

Your Answer _____

Q–539

What was the Specie Redemption Act of 1875?

Your Answer _____

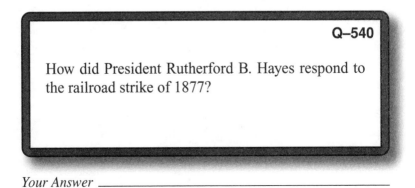

Q–540

How did President Rutherford B. Hayes respond to the railroad strike of 1877?

Your Answer _____

Correct Answers

A–538

The demonetization of silver

A–539

The Specie Redemption Act called for retiring the greenbacks and adopting the gold standard for money by 1879.

A–540

He used federal troops to restore order after numerous strikers were killed.

Questions

Q–541

What economic theory did Henry George advocate in *Progress and Poverty*?

Your Answer _____

Q–542

What different groups were included in the Knights of Labor? What caused the downfall of the Knights of Labor?

Your Answer _____

Q–543

What policies regarding railroads and money did farm groups advocate during the 1870s and 1880s?

Your Answer _____

Correct Answers

A–541

A single tax on land as the means to redistribute wealth

A–542

1) White native male workers, immigrants, women, and African Americans
2) The Haymarket Square Riot in Chicago in 1886

A–543

They wanted government regulation of railroads, currency inflation, and the use of both gold and silver.

Questions

Q–544

What was the economic effect of monopolies, and how did smaller businesses, farmers, and workers respond to monopolies?

Your Answer _____

Q–545

What abuses did many railroads practice during the 1870s and 1880s?

Your Answer _____

Q–546

What three industries developed in the South during the 1880s?

Your Answer _____

Correct Answers

A–544

Monopolies lessen competition, and so smaller businesses, farmers, and workers wanted government regulation of industries.

A–545

They fixed prices, demanded kickbacks, and set discriminatory freight rates.

A–546

Textiles, steel, and tobacco

Q–547

What happened to farm acreage and prices between 1870 and 1890?

Your Answer _____

_____

Q–548

Who founded the American Federation of Labor, what unions was it composed of, and what were its goals?

Your Answer _____

_____

Q–549

Who developed scientific management?

Your Answer _____

_____

Correct Answers

A–547

Acreage more than doubled, while many prices fell as a result of surplus production.

A–548

1) Samuel Gompers and Adolph Strasser
2) Craft unions
3) Higher wages, shorter hours, and improved safety conditions

A–549

Frederick W. Taylor

Questions

Q–550

What economic policy did Benjamin Harrison advocate in his 1888 presidential campaign?

Your Answer _____

_____

Q–551

What were trusts?

Your Answer _____

_____

Q–552

What did the Sherman Anti-Trust Act of 1890 provide?

Your Answer _____

_____

Correct Answers

A–550

A high protective tariff

A–551

Corporate monopolies

A–552

The Sherman Anti-Trust Act subjected trusts that controlled whole industries to federal prosecution if they were in restraint of trade.

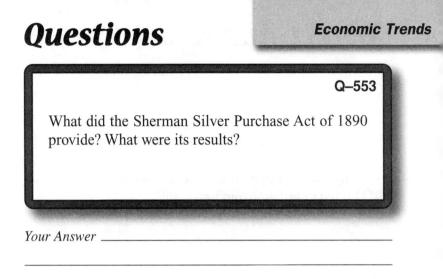

Q–553

What did the Sherman Silver Purchase Act of 1890 provide? What were its results?

Your Answer _____

_____

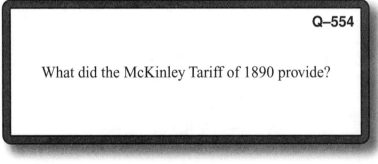

Q–554

What did the McKinley Tariff of 1890 provide?

Your Answer _____

_____

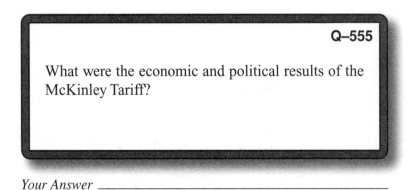

Q–555

What were the economic and political results of the McKinley Tariff?

Your Answer _____

_____

Correct Answers

A–553

1) The Sherman Silver Purchase Act called for the purchase of 4.5 million ounces of silver each month at market prices and for the backing of Treasury notes by both gold and silver.
2) It led to inflation and lower gold reserves.

A–554

The McKinley Tariff extended the protective tariff to agricultural and industrial goods and also provided for reciprocal trade agreements.

A–555

Prices went up, and the Republicans lost the 1890 congressional election.

Q–556

What was the Homestead Strike of 1892?

Your Answer _____

_____

Q–557

What percent of the work force was unemployed as a result of the Depression of 1893?

Your Answer _____

_____

Q–558

Who was Eugene Debs?

Your Answer _____

_____

Correct Answers

A–556

A strike by iron and steel workers against the Carnegie Corporation in which Andrew Carnegie hired strike-breaking Pinkerton security guards, which resulted in people on both sides being killed

A–557

20 percent

A–558

Leader of the American Railway Union

Q–559

What was the outcome of the Pullman strike of 1894?

Your Answer _____

Q–560

Why did the nation's financial centers oppose war with Spain in 1898?

Your Answer _____

Q–561

What made federal intervention in the 1902 coal strike different from previous strikes?

Your Answer _____

Correct Answers

A–559

President Grover Cleveland used federal troops to break the strike. The settlement demonstrated the power of the U.S. government to intervene against strikes that were a threat to public interest.

A–560

They favored domestic product market development over wartime production.

A–561

The 1902 intervention was the first time that the federal government intervened in a labor dispute without automatically siding with management.

Questions

Q–562

What banking reform came out of the Panic of 1907?

Your Answer _____

_____

Q–563

Who were Industrial Workers of the World (aka Wobblies)? Who was its leader? In what industries were they successful during the 1910s?

Your Answer _____

_____

Q–564

What were the economic results of World War I in Europe?

Your Answer _____

_____

Correct Answers

A–562

Establishment of the Federal Reserve System

A–563

1) The Wobblies were members of a radical labor organization.
2) "Mother" Mary Harris Jones
3) They had some success in the textile industry and western mining.

A–564

A general decline that led to the Crash of 1929 and the Great Depression of the 1930s

Q–565

When was the Federal Reserve Act passed? What was the purpose of creating a new currency called Federal Reserve Notes? What mechanism was created to supervise the Federal Reserve System?

Your Answer _____

_____

Q–566

What did the Underwood-Simmons Tariff Act of 1913 accomplish?

Your Answer _____

_____

Q–567

The Clayton Antitrust Act of 1914 was intended to supplement an existing piece of legislation. What was the name of the legislation? How did the Clayton Act affect the organization of corporations?

Your Answer _____

_____

Correct Answers

A–565

1) The Federal Reserve Act was passed in 1913.
2) The currency was designed to expand and contract with the volume of business activity and borrowing.
3) The Federal Reserve Board was created to supervise the system.

A–566

The Underwood-Simmons Tariff Act reduced average rates to about 29 percent as compared with 37 percent to 40 percent under the previous Payne-Aldrich Tariff.

A–567

1) The existing piece of legislation was the Sherman Antitrust Act.
2) Stock ownership by a corporation in a competing corporation was prohibited, and interlocking directorates of competing corporations were prohibited.

Questions

Q–568

What did the Federal Trade Commission Act of 1914 do?

Your Answer _____

_____

Q–569

What did the Child Labor Act of 1916 do? Why was the law especially significant? What happened to the law in 1918?

Your Answer _____

_____

Q–570

What factor contributed to the increased number of strikes in 1919? In what city did the police strike? Why did public support for striking workers diminish?

Your Answer _____

_____

Correct Answers

A–568

The law prohibited all unfair trade practices without defining them, and created a commission of five members appointed by the president. The commission was empowered to issue cease and desist orders to corporations, stop actions considered to be in restraint of trade, and bring lawsuits if the orders were not obeyed.

A–569

1) The Child Labor Act of 1916 forbade shipment in interstate commerce of products whose production involved the labor of children under fourteen or sixteen, depending on the product.
2) The law was especially significant because it was the first time that Congress regulated labor within a state using the interstate commerce power.
3) The law was declared unconstitutional by the Supreme Court in 1918 on the grounds that it interfered with the powers of the states.

A–570

1) The rapid postwar inflation contributed to the striking workers demand for higher wages.
2) Boston
3) The Communist Revolution of 1917 in Russia inspired in many Americans a fear of violence and revolution by workers.

Q–571

Why did coal workers strike in 1919? How was the issue resolved?

Your Answer _____

_____

Q–572

What was a major factor behind the recession of the 1920s?

Your Answer _____

_____

Q–573

What was the major reason for the improved economy during most of the 1920s?

Your Answer _____

_____

Correct Answers

A–571

1) The workers were seeking shorter hours and higher wages.
2) Attorney General Mitchell Palmer obtained injunctions and the union called off the strike. An arbitration board later awarded the miners a wage increase.

A–572

Europe returned to normal and reduced its purchases in America, and domestic demand for goods not available in wartime was filled. Prices fell and unemployment exceeded 12 percent in 1921.

A–573

Improved industrial efficiency that resulted in lower prices for goods

Q–574

The sale of what type of products was responsible for the prosperity of the 1920s?

Your Answer _____

_____

Q–575

What was the major business trend during the 1920s?

Your Answer _____

_____

Q–576

Why did farm expenses rise during the 1920s?

Your Answer _____

_____

Correct Answers

A–574

Consumer products, such as automobiles, refrigerators, and furniture

A–575

The trend toward corporate consolidation

A–576

Farm expenses rose with the cost of more sophisticated machinery and a greater use of chemical fertilizers.

Q–577

Describe President Herbert Hoover's economic philosophy.

Your Answer _____

_____

Q–578

What products were affected by the Fordney McCumber-Tariff? What year was it passed?

Your Answer _____

_____

Q–579

Give one reason for the stock market crash of 1929 and the Great Depression that followed.

Your Answer _____

_____

Correct Answers

A–577

Hoover believed that an economic system with voluntary cooperation of business and government would enable the United States to abolish poverty through continued economic growth.

A–578

1) The Fordney-McCumber Tariff imposed high rates on farm products and protected such infant industries as rayon, china, toys, and chemicals.
2) 1922

A–579

Many people had bought stock on a margin of 10 percent, meaning that they had borrowed 90 percent of the purchase through a broker's loan and put up the stock as collateral.

Questions

Q–580

Describe five economic effects of the Depression.

Your Answer _____

_____

Q–581

What was the Hawley-Smoot Tariff? When was it passed? Why is it still considered controversial?

Your Answer _____

_____

Q–582

What was the purpose of the Reconstruction Finance Corporation (RFC)?

Your Answer _____

_____

Correct Answers

A–580

1) Unemployment rose to 25 percent.
2) National income dropped 54 percent.
3) Labor income fell about 41 percent.
4) Industrial production dropped about 51 percent.
5) By 1932, 22 percent of the nation's banks had failed.

A–581

1) The Hawley-Smoot Tariff raised duties on both agricultural and manufacturer imports.
2) June 1930
3) Historians still argue over whether or not it contributed to the spread of the international depression.

A–582

Chartered by Congress in 1932, the RFC made loans to railroads, banks, and other financial institutions. Its aim was to prevent the failure of basic firms on which many other elements of the economy depended.

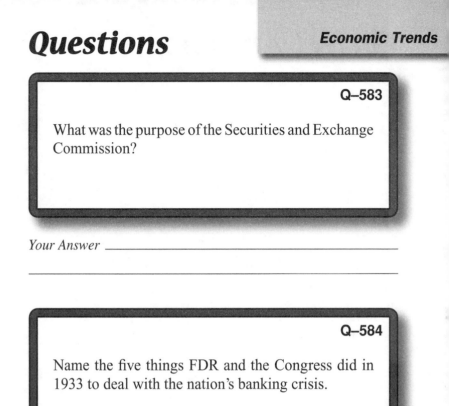

Q–583

What was the purpose of the Securities and Exchange Commission?

Your Answer _____

_____

Q–584

Name the five things FDR and the Congress did in 1933 to deal with the nation's banking crisis.

Your Answer _____

_____

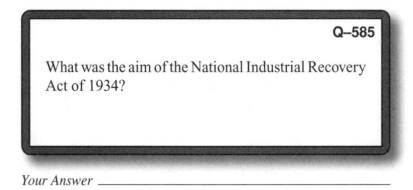

Q–585

What was the aim of the National Industrial Recovery Act of 1934?

Your Answer _____

_____

Correct Answers

A–583

To supervise stock exchanges and to punish fraud in securities trading

---

A–584

1) Passed the Emergency Banking Relief Act
2) Passed The Banking Act of 1933
3) Passed The Truth in Securities Act
4) Established the Home Owners Loan Corporation
5) Took the nation off the gold standard

A–585

The National Industrial Recovery Act of 1934 sought to stabilize the economy by preventing extreme competition, labor-management conflicts, and overproduction.

Q-586

What was the Wagner Act? When was it enacted?

Your Answer _____

_____

Q-587

What was the effect of the first New Deal policies on unemployment?

Your Answer _____

_____

Q-588

What was another term used to describe the Fair Labor Standards Act?

Your Answer _____

_____

Correct Answers

A–586

1) The Wagner Act reaffirmed labor's right to unionize, prohibited unfair labor practices, and created the National Labor Relations Board (NLRB) to oversee and ensure fairness in labor-management relations.
2) May 1935

A–587

Unemployment dropped from about 25 percent of nonfarm workers in 1933 to about 20 percent in 1935, but this unemployment rate was still much higher than the 3.2 percent of pre-Depression 1929.

A–588

The minimum wage law

Q–589

What prompted President Franklin Roosevelt to issue an executive order establishing the Fair Employment Practice Committee in June of 1941? What was the purpose of the committee?

Your Answer _____

_____

Q–590

What prompted the division in the labor movement between the American Federation of Labor (AFL) and the Congress of Industrial Organizations (CIO)?

Your Answer _____

_____

Q–591

By 1941, how many workers belonged to a union?

Your Answer _____

_____

Correct Answers

A–589

1) Black union leader A. Philip Randolph threatened to lead a black march on Washington to demand equal access to defense jobs.
2) The purpose of the committee was to ensure consideration for minorities in defense employment.

A–590

The CIO wanted to unionize the mass production industries, such as automobiles and rubber, with industrial unions while the AFL continued to try to organize workers in those industries by crafts.

A–591

8.7 million, or 41 percent of the workforce

Q–592

How did the 1947 Taft-Hartley Act affect unions?

Your Answer

Q–593

How much did economic productivity increase between 1945 and 1955?

Your Answer

Q–594

What was the minimum wage in 1955?

Your Answer

Correct Answers

A–592

The Taft-Hartley Act made the "closed shop" illegal; ended the practice of employers collecting dues for unions; and forbade such actions as secondary boycotts, jurisdictional strikes, and featherbedding.

A–593

35 percent

A–594

$1 an hour

Questions

Q–595

What was a popular critique of corporate culture in the 1950s?

Your Answer _____

_____

Q–596

Who unionized Mexican-American farmworkers?

Your Answer _____

_____

Q–597

What factors contributed to the economic slump of the early 1970s?

Your Answer _____

_____

Correct Answers

A–595

That such environments encouraged the managerial personality and corporate cooperation rather than individualism

A–596

Cesar Chavez

A–597

1) Federal deficits
2) International competition
3) Rising energy costs

Questions

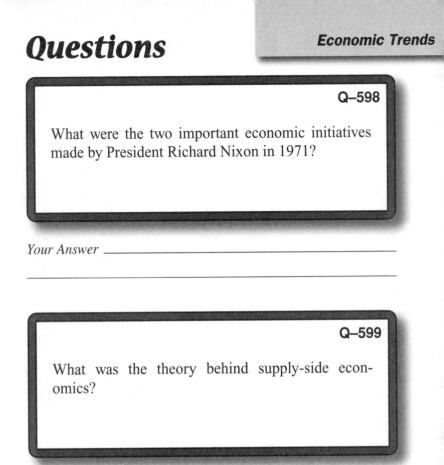

Q–598

What were the two important economic initiatives made by President Richard Nixon in 1971?

Your Answer _____

_____

Q–599

What was the theory behind supply-side economics?

Your Answer _____

_____

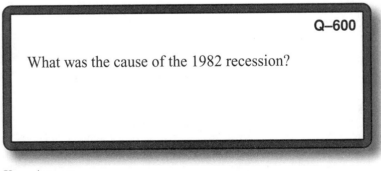

Q–600

What was the cause of the 1982 recession?

Your Answer _____

_____

Correct Answers

A-598

Nixon announced a ninety-day price and wage freeze, and he took the United States off the gold standard.

A-599

If government left more money in the hands of the people, they would invest rather than spend the excess on consumer goods. The results would be greater production, more jobs, and greater prosperity.

A-600

The Federal Reserve's "tight money" policy

Questions

Q–601

What antiunion measure did President Ronald Reagan take in 1981?

Your Answer _____

_____

Q–602

What were the major provisions of the Tax Reform Act of 1986?

Your Answer _____

_____

Q–603

What was the inflation rate in 1986?

Your Answer _____

_____

Correct Answers

A–601

He fired all striking air-traffic controllers.

A–602

The Tax Reform Act of 1986 lowered tax rates, changing the highest rate on personal income from 50 percent to 28 percent and corporate taxes from 46 percent to 34 percent. At the same time, it removed many tax shelters and tax credits.

A–603

22 percent

Questions

Q–604

What explains the rising U.S. trade deficits of the 1980s?

Your Answer _____

_____

Q–605

What explains the corporate merger phenomenon of the 1980s?

Your Answer _____

_____

Q–606

What happened on October 19, 1987, also known as "Black Monday"?

Your Answer _____

_____

Correct Answers

A–604

U.S. management and engineering skills had fallen behind Japan and Germany, and the United States provided an open market to foreign businesses.

A–605

1) Deregulation policies of the Reagan administration
2) The emerging international economy
3) Availability of funds released by new tax breaks

A–606

The Dow Jones stock market average dropped over 500 points.

Questions

Q–607

What was the cause of the financial problems of the savings and loan industry in the late 1980s?

Your Answer _____

_____

Q–608

What factors explain the drop in labor union membership in the 1980s?

Your Answer _____

_____

Q–609

In what ways does the Federal Reserve try to regulate the economy?

Your Answer _____

_____

Correct Answers

A–607

Bad real estate loans

A–608

The economy was shifting from heavy industry to electronics and service industries.

A–609

The Federal Reserve will lower interest rates to stimulate the economy and raise interest rates to regulate inflation.

Questions

Q–610

What is NAFTA? Who were its most prominent critics?

Your Answer _____

_____

Q–611

In 1994, how did the Federal Reserve respond to the fears of increased inflation?

Your Answer _____

_____

Q–612

What was the unemployment rate at the end of 1993? Why was that significant?

Your Answer _____

_____

Correct Answers

A–610

1) The North American Free Trade Agreement eliminated most tariffs and other trade barriers between the United States, Canada, and Mexico.
2) Organized labor and Ross Perot

A–611

By beginning a series of interest rate increases

A–612

1) 6.4 percent
2) It was the lowest rate since January of 1991.

Q–613

The new continent discovered by Christopher Columbus was named after _____ _____.

Your Answer _____

Q–614

True or False: John Cabot was the first explorer to reach the mainland of North America.

Your Answer _____

Q–615

Who was the first European to see the Pacific Ocean?

Your Answer _____

Correct Answers

A–613

Amerigo Vespucci

A–614

True

A–615

Vasco Nunez de Balboa

Q–616

Which explorer sought to find the fabled fountain of youth?

Your Answer _____

_____

Q–617

Which explorer led three expeditions to the St. Lawrence River, in search of the Northwest Passage?

Your Answer _____

_____

Q–618

What river in the southeastern part of the United States was discovered by Hernando de Soto?

Your Answer _____

_____

Correct Answers

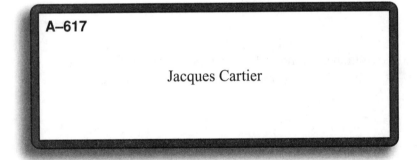

A–616

Juan Ponce de Leon

A–617

Jacques Cartier

A–618

The Mississippi River

Questions

Q–619

What explorer led an expedition from the Rio Grande in Mexico, across Arizona, New Mexico, Texas, Oklahoma, and Kansas?

Your Answer _____

_____

Q–620

Who was Sir Francis Drake?

Your Answer _____

_____

Q–621

For which country did explorer Henry Hudson set out to find the Northwest Passage?

Your Answer _____

_____

Correct Answers

A–619

Francisco Vasquez de Coronado

A–620

Sir Francis Drake was a successful English captain who sailed around South America, raided Spanish settlements on the Pacific Coast of Central America, and claimed California for England.

A–621

Holland

Questions

Q–622

Which river served as the French gateway to the interior of North America?

Your Answer _____

_____

Q–623

Who explored the Mississippi Valley in 1673?

Your Answer _____

_____

Q–624

Who designed the city of Washington, D.C.?

Your Answer _____

_____

Correct Answers

A–622

The St. Lawrence River

A–623

Jacques Marquette

A–624

Pierre L'Enfant

Q–625

Approximately what percentage of the U.S. population lived in cities in 1790?

Your Answer _____

Q–626

Who led the expedition to explore the western territory to the Pacific in 1804?

Your Answer _____

Q–627

The prevailing farming technique used in the first half of the nineteenth century was a _____ and _____ method that was wasteful of timber and diminished the fertility of the soil.

Your Answer _____

Correct Answers

A–625

5 percent

A–626

Meriwether Lewis and William Clark

A–627

clearing and planting

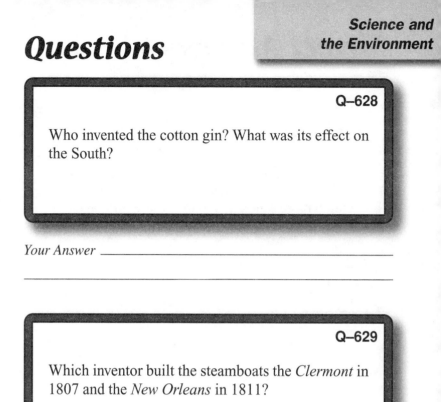

Q–628

Who invented the cotton gin? What was its effect on the South?

Your Answer _____

Q–629

Which inventor built the steamboats the *Clermont* in 1807 and the *New Orleans* in 1811?

Your Answer _____

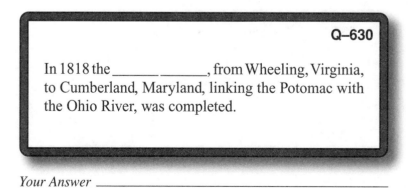

Q–630

In 1818 the _____ _____, from Wheeling, Virginia, to Cumberland, Maryland, linking the Potomac with the Ohio River, was completed.

Your Answer _____

Correct Answers

A–628

1) Eli Whitney created the cotton gin, which created a faster and more efficient means to separate the cotton fibers from the seeds.
2) This machine made the use of slave labor to farm cotton more efficient and thus more profitable.

A–629

Robert Fulton

A–630

National Road

Q–631

What major waterway system linked the Hudson River at Albany, New York, with Lake Erie?

Your Answer _____

Q–632

True or False: The canal system that was built in the first part of the nineteenth century generally ran in a north-south direction.

Your Answer _____

Q–633

What three epidemics were prevalent in urban areas of the 1830s and 1840s?

Your Answer _____

Correct Answers

A–631

The Erie Canal

A–632

False. The canals ran east-west, linking the old East with the new West.

A–633

1) Typhoid fever
2) Typhus
3) Cholera

Q–634

Who discovered a process for vulcanizing rubber?

Your Answer _____

_____

Q–635

Who invented the sewing machine?

Your Answer _____

_____

Q–636

What invention by Samuel Morse was first used in 1840 to transmit business news and information?

Your Answer _____

_____

Correct Answers

A–634

Charles Goodyear

A–635

Elias Howe

A–636

The electric telegraph

Q–637

How did industry reinforce farming?

Your Answer _____

_____

Q–638

How did Cyrus McCormick's mechanical reaper benefit the wheat farmers?

Your Answer _____

_____

Q–639

Who invented the steel plow?

Your Answer _____

_____

Correct Answers

A–637

Many of industry's technological developments and inventions were applied to farm machinery, which in turn enabled farmers to produce more food more cheaply.

A–638

The mechanical reaper enabled a crew of six men to harvest as much wheat in one day as fifteen men using older methods.

A–639

John Deere

Questions

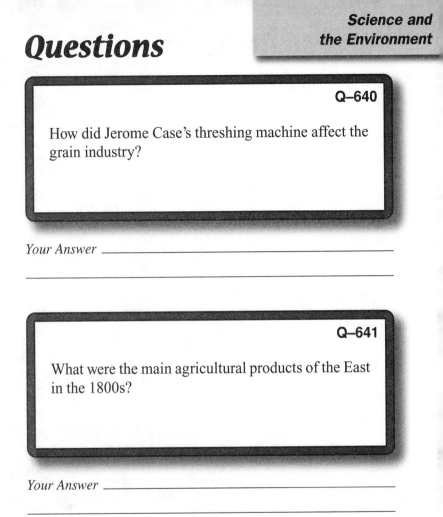

Q–640

How did Jerome Case's threshing machine affect the grain industry?

Your Answer _____

_____

Q–641

What were the main agricultural products of the East in the 1800s?

Your Answer _____

_____

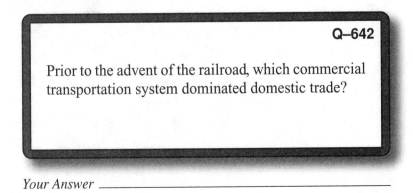

Q–642

Prior to the advent of the railroad, which commercial transportation system dominated domestic trade?

Your Answer _____

_____

Correct Answers

A–640

The threshing machine multiplied the bushels of grain that could be separated from the stalk in a day's time.

A–641

Production of milk, fruits, and berries

A–642

Coastal sailing ships

Questions

Q–643

Which states contained the most miles of railroad track?

Your Answer _____

Q–644

What were the revenue-producing crops produced by the southern plantation system—cotton, tobacco, and so on—collectively known as?

Your Answer _____

Q–645

Why did the southern population move to the newly opened Gulf States?

Your Answer _____

Correct Answers

A–643

Pennsylvania and New York

A–644

Cash crops

A–645

They could grow cotton and sugar cane in these areas.

Questions

Q–646

What did the phrase "manifest destiny" mean?

Your Answer _____

Q–647

What was the starting point of the Oregon Trail?

Your Answer _____

Q–648

What was "Oregon Fever" of the 1840s?

Your Answer _____

Correct Answers

A–646

Manifest destiny was a belief that it was the destiny of the United States to expand its territory over the whole North American continent.

A–647

Independence, Missouri

A–648

Thousands of settlers trekked across the Great Plains and the Rocky Mountains to settle in what they considered to be a new Shangri-la.

Q–649

Why did Great Britain want the Puget Sound area north of the Columbia River in the Oregon Territory?

Your Answer _____

_____

Q–650

What were the terms of the Gadsden Purchase? What was its purpose?

Your Answer _____

_____

Q–651

What territory did President Franklin Pierce try to purchase in the Ostend Manifesto?

Your Answer _____

_____

Correct Answers

A–649

Because Puget Sound is one of only three natural harbors on the Pacific Coast

A–650

1) The United States bought from Mexico a strip of land along the Gila River in what is now southern New Mexico and Arizona.
2) Its purpose was to provide a good route for a transcontinental railroad across the southern part of the United States.

A–651

He tried to purchase Cuba from Spain.

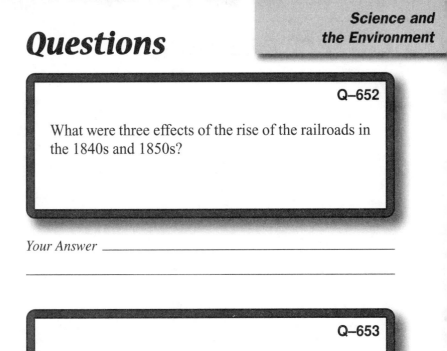

Q–652

What were three effects of the rise of the railroads in the 1840s and 1850s?

Your Answer _____

_____

Q–653

What means of transportation were popular on the rivers and seas in the 1850s?

Your Answer _____

_____

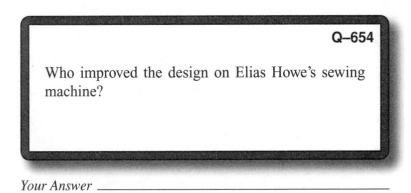

Q–654

Who improved the design on Elias Howe's sewing machine?

Your Answer _____

_____

Correct Answers

A–652

1) Big-business techniques spread.
2) A nationwide market developed.
3) The Midwest became linked to the North rather than to the South.

A–653

1) Steamboats
2) Clipper ships

A–654

Isaac Singer improved Howe's design and built the first commercially successful sewing machine.

Q–655

What were the main products of midwestern family farms in the 1850s?

Your Answer _____

_____

Q–656

Why did the North, unlike the South, face incentives to develop labor-saving machines?

Your Answer _____

_____

Q–657

What two labor-saving machines were midwestern farmers using by 1860?

Your Answer _____

_____

Correct Answers

A–655

Grain and livestock

A–656

The North did not have an abundant source of cheap labor, that is, slaves.

A–657

Cyrus McCormick's mechanical reaper and the mechanical thresher

Questions

Q–658

Why was John C. Fremont known as "the Pathfinder"?

Your Answer _____

_____

Q–659

What major technological innovation in naval warfare took place during the Civil War?

Your Answer _____

_____

Q–660

Who was Alexander Graham Bell?

Your Answer _____

_____

Correct Answers

A–658

Because of his explorations in the Rockies and the Far West

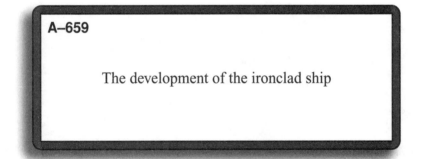

A–659

The development of the ironclad ship

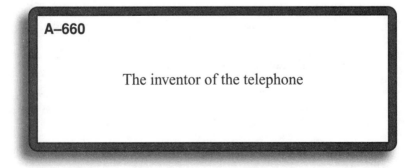

A–660

The inventor of the telephone

Questions

Q–661

What did Thomas Edison invent?

Your Answer _____

Q–662

Who was Elisha Otis, and what influence did he have on urban growth?

Your Answer _____

Q–663

What well-known agricultural chemist studied at Tuskegee Institute?

Your Answer _____

Correct Answers

A–661

Edison invented electrical devices, including the incandescent lamp, the mimeograph, and the phonograph.

A–662

Otis was the inventor of the mechanical elevator, which led to the development of the skyscraper.

A–663

George Washington Carver

Questions

Q–664

What was the effect of the invention of the linotype machine?

Your Answer _____

_____

Q–665

In what industry was the moving assembly line first introduced?

Your Answer _____

_____

Q–666

Who was the first American to win a Nobel Prize, and what did he win it for?

Your Answer _____

_____

Correct Answers

A–664

The linotype machine cut printing costs dramatically and led to the rise of the publishing industry.

A–665

The moving assembly line was introduced in the automobile industry by Henry Ford in 1913 and 1914.

A–666

Physicist Albert Michelson won for his work on the speed of light.

Questions

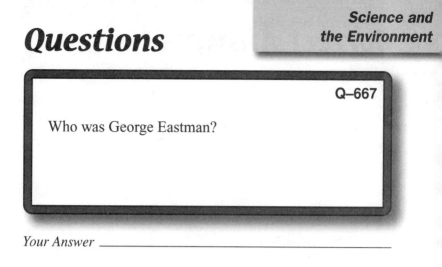

Q–667

Who was George Eastman?

Your Answer _____

_____

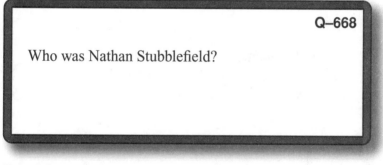

Q–668

Who was Nathan Stubblefield?

Your Answer _____

_____

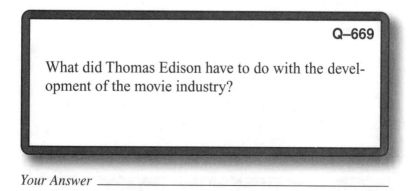

Q–669

What did Thomas Edison have to do with the development of the movie industry?

Your Answer _____

_____

Correct Answers

A–667

George Eastman was the inventor of the roll-film camera.

A–668

Nathan Stubblefield was an inventor who transmitted the human voice over the air without wires in 1892, leading to the invention of the radio.

A–669

Edison, along with his lab photographer, W. K. L. Dickson, and other assistants, invented the kinetoscope, which permitted the viewing of motion pictures.

Questions

Q–670

What were some actions taken by Theodore Roosevelt's administration with regard to conservation?

Your Answer _____

_____

Q–671

What did the Wright brothers invent?

Your Answer _____

_____

Q–672

Where was an isthmian canal proposed? Where did the United States build the canal? When did the canal open?

Your Answer _____

_____

Correct Answers

A–670

A number of national parks, forests, and irrigation projects were created; water power was developed; and the National Conservation Commission was set up to oversee the nation's natural resources.

A–671

The airplane

A–672

1) Nicaragua and Panama
2) Panama
3) 1914

Questions

Q–673

Who was Henry Ford?

Your Answer _____

_____

Q–674

Who was William Coolidge?

Your Answer _____

_____

Q–675

Who was Robert Goddard?

Your Answer _____

_____

Correct Answers

A–673

Henry Ford was an automobile manufacturer who introduced the continuous flow process on the automobile assembly line.

A–674

William Coolidge was the inventor of the X-ray tube.

A–675

Robert Goddard was the developer of liquid rocket fuel.

Q–676

What did Arthur Little invent in 1909?

Your Answer _____

_____

Q–677

What did Leo Baekeland invent in 1909?

Your Answer _____

_____

Q–678

What improvement in submarines did Adolph Busch develop?

Your Answer _____

_____

Correct Answers

A–676

Rayon

A–677

Plastics

A–678

Busch applied the diesel engine to the submarine.

Questions

Q–679

What scientist is credited with producing the first atomic chain reaction?

Your Answer _____

_____

Q–680

What was the Manhattan Project?

Your Answer _____

_____

Q–681

Where was the first atomic bomb exploded? When was it exploded?

Your Answer _____

_____

Correct Answers

A–679

Enrico Fermi of the University of Chicago

A–680

The Manhattan Project was established in August 1942 for the purpose of developing an atomic bomb.

A–681

1) Alamogordo, New Mexico
2) July 16, 1945

Questions

Q–682

What did the Atomic Energy Act of 1954 do?

Your Answer _____

_____

Q–683

When did the Soviet Union launch *Sputnik*? What were some of the consequences in the United States?

Your Answer _____

_____

Q–684

Who were the first men to walk on the moon? When?

Your Answer _____

_____

Correct Answers

A–682

The Atomic Energy Act allowed the construction of private nuclear power plants under Atomic Energy Commission license and oversight.

A–683

1) October 4, 1957
2) The launch of the Sputnik satellite created fear that the United States was falling behind technologically, and as a result, in 1958 Congress established the National Aeronautics and Space Administration (NASA) to coordinate research and development, and passed the National Defense Education Act to provide grants and loans for education.

A–684

1) Neil Armstrong and Edwin (Buzz) Aldrin
2) July 20, 1969

Questions

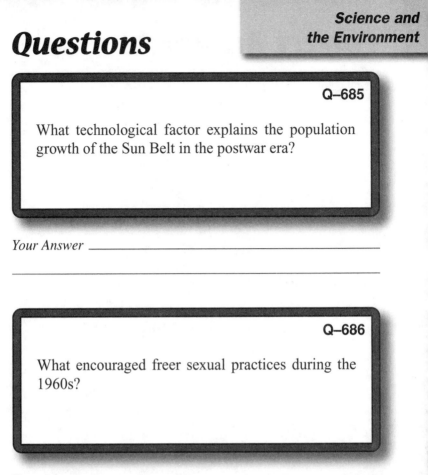

Q–685

What technological factor explains the population growth of the Sun Belt in the postwar era?

Your Answer _____

_____

Q–686

What encouraged freer sexual practices during the 1960s?

Your Answer _____

_____

Q–687

What was the Nuclear Test Ban Treaty?

Your Answer _____

_____

Correct Answers

A–685

Increased use of air conditioning

A–686

New methods of birth control, particularly the "pill"

A–687

The Nuclear Test Ban Treaty, which was signed in 1963 by all major powers except France and China, banned the atmospheric testing of nuclear weapons.

Questions

Q–688

What new, potent illegal drug appeared in the 1980s?

Your Answer _____

_____

Q–689

When was AIDS discovered? Who were its primary victims?

Your Answer _____

_____

Q–690

What event in 1986 damaged NASA's credibility?

Your Answer _____

_____

Correct Answers

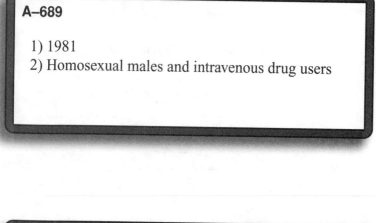

A–688

Crack cocaine

A–689

1) 1981
2) Homosexual males and intravenous drug users

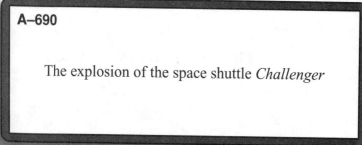

A–690

The explosion of the space shuttle *Challenger*

Questions

Q–691

What happened to the *Exxon Valdez* in 1989? How was the incident resolved?

Your Answer _____

_____

Q–692

What was the objective of the 1990 Clean Air Act? What were some of its provisions?

Your Answer _____

_____

Q–693

What doctor became associated with the issue of assisted suicide for the terminally ill in the 1990s?

Your Answer _____

_____

Correct Answers

A–691

1) The *Exxon Valdez* spilled more than 240,000 barrels of oil into Alaska's Prince William Sound in March of 1989.
2) Exxon was required to pay $1.025 billion in fines and restitution through the year 2001.

A–692

1) To reduce the level of emissions by 50 percent by the year 2000
2) Cleaner gasolines were to be developed, cities were to reduce ozone, and nitrogen oxide emissions were to be cut by one-third.

A–693

Dr. Jack Kevorkian

Q–694

How did the Food and Drug Administration respond in 1994 to the growing concern over the negative effects of dietary fat?

Your Answer ⎯⎯⎯⎯⎯⎯⎯⎯⎯⎯⎯⎯⎯⎯⎯

⎯⎯⎯⎯⎯⎯⎯⎯⎯⎯⎯⎯⎯⎯⎯⎯⎯⎯⎯

Q–695

What is the name of the telescope placed into orbit around the Earth in 1990?

Your Answer ⎯⎯⎯⎯⎯⎯⎯⎯⎯⎯⎯⎯⎯⎯⎯

⎯⎯⎯⎯⎯⎯⎯⎯⎯⎯⎯⎯⎯⎯⎯⎯⎯⎯⎯

Q–696

Who won the Nobel Peace Prize in 2007 for his efforts to raise awareness about global warming?

Your Answer ⎯⎯⎯⎯⎯⎯⎯⎯⎯⎯⎯⎯⎯⎯⎯

⎯⎯⎯⎯⎯⎯⎯⎯⎯⎯⎯⎯⎯⎯⎯⎯⎯⎯⎯

Correct Answers

A–694

By requiring food manufacturers to use new labeling on packaged foods, which gave the percentage per serving of the recommended daily amounts for various substances including fats.

A–695

The Hubble Space Telescope

A–696

Al Gore was awarded the Nobel Peace Prize in 2007 and has been instrumental in raising awareness of global warming in recent years.

STOP **Take Test-Readiness Quiz 3 on CD**
(to review questions 490-696)

Questions

Q–697

Why did Spain urge the pope to draw up a "Line of Demarcation" in the New World?

Your Answer —————————————————————

—————————————————————————————————

Q–698

Why did Spain and Portugal decide to draw up the Treaty of Tordesillas in 1493?

Your Answer —————————————————————

—————————————————————————————————

Q–699

Who were the conquistadors?

Your Answer —————————————————————

Correct Answers

A–697

The Line of Demarcation favored Spain over Portugal as Spain was entitled to all lands west of Cape Verdes Island. Portugal, however, had a stronger navy.

A–698

Spain wanted to confirm its ownership of New World lands but feared interference from Portugal, a powerful seafaring nation that had been active in overseas exploration.

A–699

Independent Spanish adventurers who led their country's army into the New World, seeking wealth, glory, and to spread the Roman Catholic faith

Questions

Q–700

Which conquistador conquered the Aztec Empire?

Your Answer _____

Q–701

Why did England and France pay little attention to America during the sixteenth century?

Your Answer _____

Q–702

What was the Protestant Reformation?

Your Answer _____

Correct Answers

A–700

Hernando Cortes

A–701

Both countries were experiencing problems caused by the Protestant Reformation.

A–702

A religious movement begun by Martin Luther, who taught that an individual's salvation was determined by faith alone, rather than the church's elaborate sacraments

Q–703

_____ _____ was a religious thinker who taught the doctrine of predestination.

Your Answer _____

Q–704

Who were the Huguenots?

Your Answer _____

Q–705

List two important consequences that followed England's defeat of the Spanish Armada.

Your Answer _____

Correct Answers

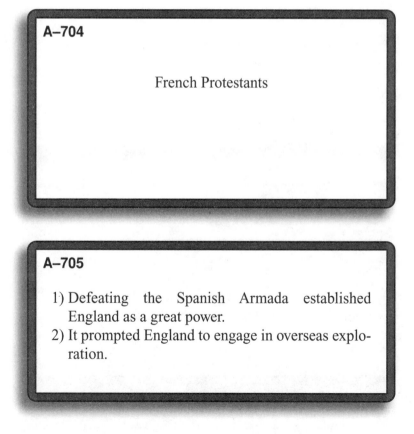

A–703

John Calvin

A–704

French Protestants

A–705

1) Defeating the Spanish Armada established England as a great power.
2) It prompted England to engage in overseas exploration.

Questions

Q–706

In which modern-day Canadian city did Samuel de Champlain set up a trading post?

Your Answer _____

Q–707

Why did the French manage to stay on relatively good terms with the Indians?

Your Answer _____

Q–708

True or False: The French established a number of real towns in the Midwest.

Your Answer _____

Correct Answers

A–706

Quebec

A–707

Relatively few Frenchmen came to America. There-
fore, they were not infringing on Indian territories.

A–708

False. French settlements consisted of forts and trading posts.

Questions

Q–709

The Dutch West India Company traded with the _____ Indians for furs.

Your Answer _____

Q–710

What was the patroon system?

Your Answer _____

Q–711

True or False: Spanish settlements spread through the Great Lakes, and the Mississippi and Ohio River Valleys.

Your Answer _____

Correct Answers

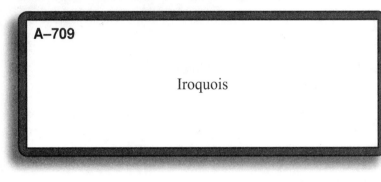

A–709

Iroquois

A–710

To keep the colony of New Netherlands supplied with food, the Dutch devised the patroon system that would award large landed estates to men who transported at least fifty families to the colony. These transported families would work as tenant farmers on the estate of the person who transported them.

A–711

False. The French established settlements in these locations.

Questions

Q–712

Which English king was restored to the British throne following the twenty-year Puritan revolution?

Your Answer _____

_____

Q–713

Which country was England's chief maritime rival during the seventeenth century?

Your Answer _____

_____

Q–714

In general, why did American colonists dislike the Navigation Acts?

Your Answer _____

_____

Correct Answers

A–712

Charles II

A–713

Holland

A–714

The Navigation Acts increased the prices that Americans had to pay for British goods and lowered the prices that Americans received for the goods they produced.

Q–715

True or False: King Philip's War took place in the Virginia Colony.

Your Answer _____

_____

Q–716

Who did James II send to head the Dominion of New England?

Your Answer _____

_____

Q–717

How did the Glorious Revolution of 1658 affect the English monarchy?

Your Answer _____

_____

Correct Answers

A–715

False. The war took place in New England.

A–716

Sir Edmund Andros

A–717

The Glorious Revolution of 1658 replaced Catholic James with his Protestant daughter Mary and her husband William of Orange as England's monarchs.

Questions

Q–718

Why were the Americans disappointed with the terms set forth in the Treaty of Aix-La Chapelle of 1748?

Your Answer _____

_____

Q–719

What famous young major of the Virginia militia was sent to western Pennsylvania to expel the French?

Your Answer _____

_____

Q–720

What territory did Britain gain in the Treaty of Paris (1763)?

Your Answer _____

_____

Correct Answers

A–718

The British gave Louisbourg back to France in exchange for lands in India.

A–719

George Washington

A–720

All of Canada and all of the United States east of the Mississippi

Questions

Q–721

Which Ottowa chief led a bloody Indian uprising, vowing to drown the entire white population in the sea?

Your Answer _____

_____

Q–722

What was the Proclamation of 1763? Why was it issued?

Your Answer _____

_____

Q–723

True or False: Violators of the Sugar Act faced trial in admiralty courts without benefit of jury or the normal due processes of law.

Your Answer _____

_____

Correct Answers

A–721

Pontiac

A–722

1) The Proclamation of 1763 forbade whites to settle west of the Appalachians.
2) It was issued to improve Anglo-Indian relations, prevent further Indian uprisings, and keep settlers closer to the coast, where they would be more easily controlled.

A–723

True

Questions

Q–724

The _____ _____ required colonists to pay for the maintenance of British troops stationed in their area.

Your Answer _____

Q–725

What British act forbade the colonists from issuing paper money that would not be redeemable in gold or silver?

Your Answer _____

Q–726

Which British act imposed a tax on every piece of printed paper, from newspapers to legal documents, in the colonies?

Your Answer _____

Correct Answers

A–724

Quartering Act

A–725

The Currency Act of 1764

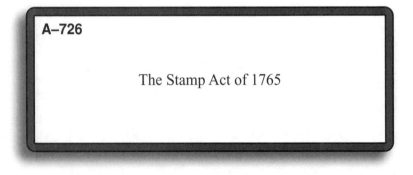

A–726

The Stamp Act of 1765

Questions

Q–727

How did the colonists initially deal with the series of British acts that were passed in the 1760s?

Your Answer _____

_____

Q–728

What was the Stamp Act Congress?

Your Answer _____

_____

Q–729

How did colonial merchants achieve the repeal of the Stamp Act?

Your Answer _____

_____

Correct Answers

A–727

The colonists used petitions and pamphlets to protest these acts.

A–728

The Stamp Act Congress consisted of delegates from nine colonies that met in 1765 and passed moderate resolutions against the Stamp Act, asserting that Americans could not be taxed without representation.

A–729

They boycotted British goods.

Questions

Q–730

What did the Declaratory Act of 1768 state?

Your Answer _____

Q–731

What main principle did the pamphlet titled *Letters from a Farmer in Pennsylvania* point out?

Your Answer _____

Q–732

Why was the Boston Massacre labeled as such by Samuel Adams when only five people were killed and it was partially incited by the colonists?

Your Answer _____

Correct Answers

A–730

The Declaratory Act of 1768 claimed the power to tax or make laws for Americans in all cases.

A–731

Letters from a Farmer in Pennsylvania pointed out that the Townshend Act violated the principle of no taxation without representation.

A–732

Adams wanted to incite the colonists to rise up against the British.

Questions

Q–733

What was the *Gaspee* Affair?

Your Answer _____

_____

Q–734

Why did the British East India Company seek a concession from Parliament that allowed it to ship tea directly to the colonies?

Your Answer _____

_____

Q–735

Why did the Americans resist buying British tea?

Your Answer _____

_____

Correct Answers

A–733

A group of Rhode Islanders dressed up as Indians and burned the *Gaspee,* a British schooner.

A–734

The British East India Company was in desperate financial straits and hoped to lower the price on its tea so that it would be cheaper than the smuggled Dutch tea.

A–735

Americans did not want the British to think that they had accepted Parliament's right to tax them.

Q–736

How did Bostonians react to Governor Thomas Hutchinson's plan to attempt to collect the tea tax? What was the British reaction to the colonists?

Your Answer _____

_____

Q–737

What were the Coercive Acts?

Your Answer _____

_____

Q–738

What was the Quebec Act? Why were Americans disappointed by it?

Your Answer _____

_____

Correct Answers

A–736

1) In the incident later called the Boston Tea Party, Boston colonists disguised themselves as Indians, boarded tea-bearing ships docked in Boston Harbor, and threw the tea overboard.
2) In response, the British passed the Boston Port Act, which closed Boston Harbor to all trade until Boston had paid for all the tea. In addition, any royal officials accused of crimes in Massachusetts would be tried elsewhere.

A–737

The Coercive Acts were Britain's response to the dumping of tea by colonists in Boston Harbor.

A–738

1) The Quebec Act extended the Province of Quebec to the Ohio River, established Roman Catholicism as Quebec's religion, and set up a government without representative assembly in Quebec.
2) American colonists were disappointed because they felt they had fought for that land for westward expansion.

Questions

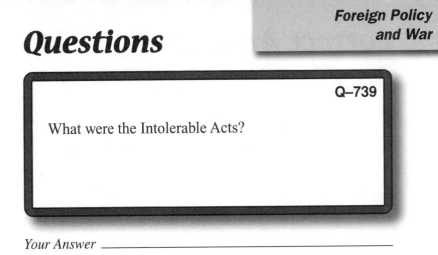

Q–739

What were the Intolerable Acts?

Your Answer _____

_____

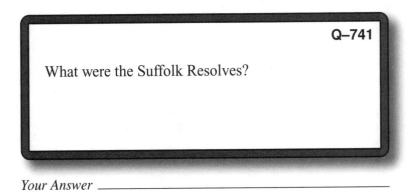

Q–740

How did Americans initially respond to the Coercive Acts?

Your Answer _____

_____

Q–741

What were the Suffolk Resolves?

Your Answer _____

_____

Correct Answers

A–739

Americans lumped the Quebec Act with the Coercive Acts and referred to them as the Intolerable Acts.

A–740

They called the First Continental Congress in September 1774.

A–741

The Suffolk Resolves denounced the Intolerable Acts and called for strict nonimportation and rigorous preparation of local militia companies in case the British should resort to military force.

Questions

Q–742

How did the British authorities react to the Americans' Continental Congress?

Your Answer _____

Q–743

What happened at Lexington and Concord?

Your Answer _____

Q–744

What was considered to be the bloodiest battle of the American Revolution?

Your Answer _____

Correct Answers

A–742

The British authorities paid little attention to the Americans' grievances and sent more troops to Massachusetts, which they determined to be in a state of rebellion.

A–743

The British marched to Concord to destroy a stock-pile of colonial weapons. News of their march was spread by riders like Paul Revere and William Dawes. Minutemen—a select group of armed militia—were waiting for the British at Lexington. A shot was fired and eight Minutemen were killed. By the time the British arrived at Concord, all supplies had been moved.

A–744

The Battle at Bunker Hill

Questions

Q–745

How did King George III respond to the colonies' petition to intercede with Parliament?

Your Answer _____

_____

Q–746

Why did the French help the Americans in its struggle against Britain?

Your Answer _____

_____

Q–747

Where was General George Washington's army forced to take up winter quarters after being driven out of Philadelphia?

Your Answer _____

_____

Correct Answers

A–745

George III declared that the colonies were in rebellion and that preparations were being made for a full-scale war against America.

A–746

The French hated Britain and saw the war as a way to weaken Britain by depriving it of its colonies.

A–747

Valley Forge

Questions

Q–748

Why was the American victory at Saratoga, New York, so important?

Your Answer _____

_____

Q–749

In addition to France, name two other countries that joined America in its war against Britain.

Your Answer _____

_____

Q–750

What was the Americans' outlook after the British victories in the South?

Your Answer _____

_____

Correct Answers

A–748

The American victory at Saratoga convinced the French to join openly in the war against England.

A–749

Holland and Spain

A–750

The Americans' outlook was poor. The British seemed to be winning the war.

Questions

Q–751

Which famous American leader went over to the British side in 1780?

Your Answer _____

_____

Q–752

What two main problems did the British naval forces face during the American Revolution?

Your Answer _____

_____

Q–753

Who was John Paul Jones?

Your Answer _____

_____

Correct Answers

A–751

Benedict Arnold

A–752

1) The British merchant marine was preyed on by the U.S. Navy and privately owned American vessels.
2) French and Spanish naval forces struck against various British empire outposts.

A–753

John Paul Jones was the most famous of the American naval leaders who captured British ships and carried out audacious raids along the coast of Britain.

Questions

Q–754

Following the American victory at Yorktown, Virginia, which three Americans made up the peace-treaty negotiating team?

Your Answer _____

_____

Q–755

What were the provisions of the Treaty of Paris that ended the American Revolution?

Your Answer _____

_____

Q–756

What territory was returned to Spain in the Treaty of Paris?

Your Answer _____

_____

Correct Answers

A–754

Benjamin Franklin, John Jay, and John Adams

A–755

America's western boundary became the Mississippi River, and Great Britain agreed to remove all of its western outposts.

A–756

Florida

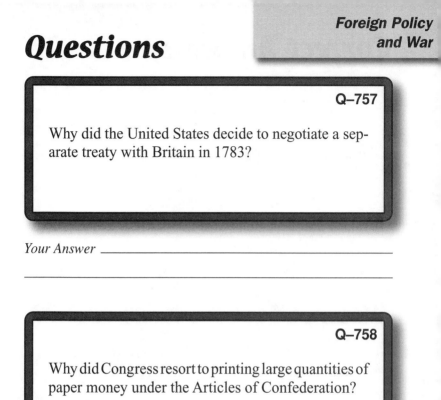

Q–757

Why did the United States decide to negotiate a separate treaty with Britain in 1783?

Your Answer _____

_____

Q–758

Why did Congress resort to printing large quantities of paper money under the Articles of Confederation?

Your Answer _____

_____

Q–759

How did the United States manage to finance the American Revolution without suffering complete economic collapse?

Your Answer _____

_____

Correct Answers

A–757

France and Spain were planning to achieve an agreement that would have been unfavorable to the United States.

A–758

Congress needed money to finance the war but was unable to tax its citizens.

A–759

France and the Netherlands lent the United States money in the form of grants and loans.

Questions

Q–760

What was Shays' Rebellion?

Your Answer _____

Q–761

What excuse did the British use for not evacuating the northwest outposts after the American Revolution?

Your Answer _____

Q–762

What was the Pinckney Treaty of 1795?

Your Answer _____

Correct Answers

A–760

Daniel Shays led a group of Massachusetts farmers to shut down the Massachusetts courts so that the judges would not be able to seize property or condemn people to debtors' prisons for not paying taxes.

A–761

The British refused to leave because the states would not comply with the Treaty of Paris's provision regarding debts and loyalist property.

A–762

The Pinckney Treaty was a treaty between Spain and the United States whereby Spain opened up the Mississippi River to American trade and recognized the 31st parallel as being the northern boundary of Florida.

Questions

Q–763

How did Americans' outrage during the XYZ Affair affect American-French trade relations?

Your Answer _____

_____

Q–764

The Louisiana Territory was sold by France to the United States for $_____ million.

Your Answer _____

_____

Q–765

Why did President Thomas Jefferson send a naval force to the Mediterranean in 1801?

Your Answer _____

_____

Correct Answers

A–763

After the XYZ Affair, President John Adams suspended trade relations with the French and authorized American ship captains to attack armed French vessels.

A–764

15

A–765

To break the practice of North African Muslim leaders exacting tribute from western merchant ships

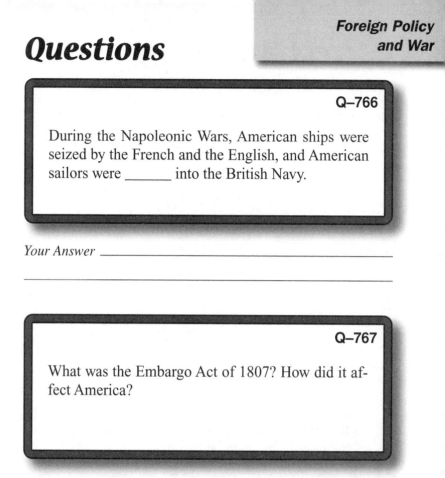

Q–766

During the Napoleonic Wars, American ships were seized by the French and the English, and American sailors were _____ into the British Navy.

Your Answer _____

_____

Q–767

What was the Embargo Act of 1807? How did it affect America?

Your Answer _____

_____

Q–768

What was the Non-Intercourse Act? What replaced it when it expired?

Your Answer _____

_____

Correct Answers

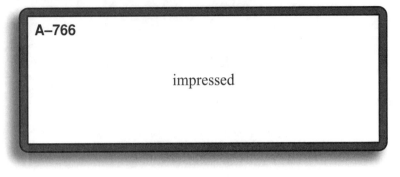

A–766

impressed

A–767

1) The Embargo Act of 1807 prohibited American ships from leaving port for any foreign destination.
2) It resulted in economic depression, especially for the heavily commercial Northeast.

A–768

1) The Non-Intercourse Act was a modified embargo act that opened trade to all nations except France and Great Britain.
2) When it expired in 1810, it was replaced with Macon's Bill No. 2, which gave the president the power to prohibit trade with any nation that violated U.S. neutrality.

Q–769

Which Shawnee Indian chief united the Mississippi Valley tribes to reestablish dominance in the old Northwest?

Your Answer _____

_____

Q–770

How did the U.S. government deal with Tecumseh and his Indian confederacy?

Your Answer _____

_____

Q–771

True or False: William Henry Harrison successfully defeated the British at the Battle of New Orleans.

Your Answer _____

_____

Correct Answers

A–769

Tecumseh

A–770

William Henry Harrison destroyed Tecumseh's village on Tippecanoe Creek and demolished Tecumseh's dream of an Indian confederacy.

A–771

False. Andrew Jackson defeated the British at New Orleans.

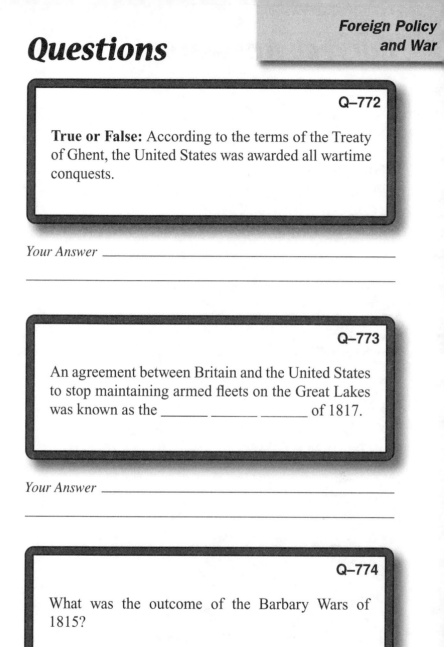

Q–772

True or False: According to the terms of the Treaty of Ghent, the United States was awarded all wartime conquests.

Your Answer _____

_____

Q–773

An agreement between Britain and the United States to stop maintaining armed fleets on the Great Lakes was known as the _____ _____ _____ of 1817.

Your Answer _____

_____

Q–774

What was the outcome of the Barbary Wars of 1815?

Your Answer _____

_____

Correct Answers

A–772

False. Both Britain and the United States returned their wartime conquests to each other, thus reestablishing the status quo that was in effect prior to the war.

A–773

Rush-Bagot Treaty

A–774

The North African pirates had to pay indemnities for past tribute they had exacted from U.S. captains, and the United States had free access to the Mediterranean Basin after this action.

Questions

Q–775

According to the _____ _____ of 1819, Spain agreed to sell the remainder of Florida to the United States.

Your Answer _____

Q–776

What message was conveyed to European powers in the Monroe Doctrine?

Your Answer _____

Q–777

What was President Andrew Jackson's policy regarding Indian tribes?

Your Answer _____

Correct Answers

A–775

Adams-Otis Treaty

A–776

The Western Hemisphere was closed to future colonization by European powers.

A–777

He supported the removal of all Indian tribes west of the Mississippi.

Q–778

What was the Trail of Tears?

Your Answer _____

Q–779

Who was the Mexican dictator that destroyed the Texas garrisons at the Alamo and at Goliad?

Your Answer _____

Q–780

What did Mexican officials do to stop the flood of American immigrants to Texas by 1836?

Your Answer _____

Correct Answers

A–778

The Trail of Tears was the forced march of thousands of Cherokees under army escort from Georgia to the West. Twenty-five percent or more of the Cherokees perished on this march.

A–779

Antonio Lopez de Santa Anna

A–780

They put restrictions on new immigration and increased taxes.

Questions

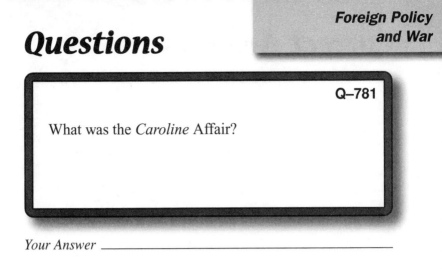

Q–781

What was the *Caroline* Affair?

Your Answer _____

_____

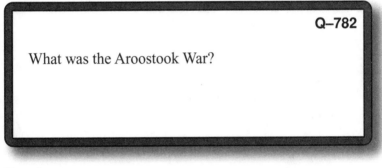

Q–782

What was the Aroostook War?

Your Answer _____

_____

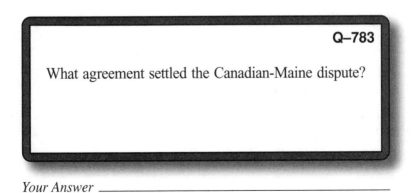

Q–783

What agreement settled the Canadian-Maine dispute?

Your Answer _____

_____

Correct Answers

A–781

The *Caroline* Affair was the burning of the USS *Caroline* by Canadian loyalists because the ship had been carrying arms to Canadian rebels.

A–782

The Aroostook War was a dispute that broke out between the people of Maine and Canadians when Canadians built a road into the forest on the Maine border.

A–783

The Webster-Ashburton Agreement of 1842, which established a border line that is still in existence today

Q–784

What happened to U.S.-British relations as a result of the Webster-Ashburton Treaty of 1842?

Your Answer _____

_____

Q–785

How did slavery cause tension between the United States and Great Britain in the early 1840s?

Your Answer _____

_____

Q–786

What was the meaning of James K. Polk's presidential campaign slogan, "Fifty-four forty or fight"?

Your Answer _____

_____

Correct Answers

A–784

Relations improved as a spirit of compromise and forbearance developed between the two nations.

A–785

Great Britain refused to return escaped slaves who had taken over a U.S. merchant ship, the *Creole,* and sailed it to the British-owned Bahamas. British ships trying to suppress slave smuggling carried out stop-and-search missions against American ships off the coast of Africa.

A–786

The slogan meant that Polk favored American annexation of the Oregon country (up to the 54' 40' north latitude line), which previously had been jointly occupied by the United States and Great Britain.

Questions

Q–787

Why was President James K. Polk reluctant to fight Great Britain over Oregon?

Your Answer _____

Q–788

How did the Oregon Treaty of 1846 settle the dispute between the United States and Great Britain?

Your Answer _____

Q–789

What was the Bear Flag Revolt?

Your Answer _____

Correct Answers

A–787

Polk was more interested in Texas, where trouble was brewing. Also, he considered Oregon unsuitable for agriculture and unavailable for slavery.

A–788

The Oregon Treaty split the disputed Oregon Territory by extending the existing U.S.-Canada boundary of the 49th parallel westward to the Pacific.

A–789

A revolt against the Mexican government by American settlers in California

Questions

Q–790

What territorial dispute between Mexico and the United States helped bring about the Mexican War?

Your Answer _____

Q–791

What did President Polk hope to accomplish by sending John Slidell to Mexico City in 1845?

Your Answer _____

Q–792

Why did some people support the Mexican War while others opposed it?

Your Answer _____

Correct Answers

A–790

The United States claimed the Rio Grande as the southern boundary of Texas, while Mexico claimed the Nueces River, 130 miles farther north, as the boundary.

A–791

Polk hoped to settle differences between the United States and Mexico peacefully.

A–792

Some people supported the war because they felt Mexico had provoked it, and it gave the United States an opportunity to spread freedom to oppressed people. Others opposed the war because they felt the United States provoked the war, or it was a war to spread slavery.

Questions

Q–793

What were the terms of the Treaty of Guadalupe-Hidalgo?

Your Answer _____

_____

Q–794

What was the political effect of the Mexican War within the United States?

Your Answer _____

_____

Q–795

Why did Commodore Matthew Perry lead a U.S. naval force into Tokyo Bay in 1853?

Your Answer _____

_____

Correct Answers

A–793

Mexico ceded southern Texas, California, and other territories in the far West to the United States in exchange for $15 million and the assumption of claims by American citizens against the Mexican government.

A–794

The Mexican War brought to the surface the issue of slavery in the new territories.

A–795

To open Japan, which previously had been closed to the outside world, to American diplomacy and trade

Questions

Q–796

Which southern state was the first to secede from the Union?

Your Answer _____

_____

Q–797

Who was the first and only president of the Confederate States?

Your Answer _____

_____

Q–798

What did the Confederate constitution say concerning state sovereignty?

Your Answer _____

_____

Correct Answers

A–796

South Carolina

A–797

Jefferson Davis

A–798

The Confederate constitution recognized the sovereignty of the states rather than that of the Confederacy.

Questions

Q–799

How did President James Buchanan respond to the establishment of the Confederate States, and why?

Your Answer _____

_____

Q–800

What did President Abraham Lincoln say about secession in his inaugural address in 1861?

Your Answer _____

_____

Q–801

How did President Lincoln respond to the Confederate firing on Fort Sumter?

Your Answer _____

_____

Correct Answers

A–799

Buchanan did nothing on the grounds that although it was unconstitutional for states to secede, it was likewise unconstitutional for the federal government to do anything about secession.

A–800

Lincoln urged southerners to reconsider and said that states had no right to secede. He announced that the federal government would continue to hold forts and military installations in the South.

A–801

Lincoln declared the existence of an insurrection and called for 75,000 volunteers to put it down.

Q–802

How did President Lincoln prevent Maryland from seceding?

Your Answer _____

_____

Q–803

At the onset of the Civil War, how did the North and South compare in terms of wealth, industry, manpower, navy, and railway system?

Your Answer _____

_____

Q–804

What advantages did the South have at the onset of the Civil War?

Your Answer _____

_____

Correct Answers

A–802

Lincoln suspended the writ of habeas corpus and declared martial law.

A–803

1) The North was much wealthier and more able to fund the war.
2) The North was more industrialized and better able to produce war materials.
3) The North had around three times as many people.
4) The North had control of the navy so it could blockade the South.
5) Unlike the South, the North's railway system was complete with a unified gauge.

A–804

The South was fighting a defensive war, and so they just had to keep the North from winning. The South was also very large, which made it difficult to conquer and control. The South also had far superior military leaders.

Questions

Q–805

What did the first Battle of Bull Run show about the two sides and the probable length of the war?

Your Answer _____

_____

Q–806

What was the Anaconda Plan?

Your Answer _____

_____

Q–807

What was the result of the North's naval blockade of the South?

Your Answer _____

_____

Correct Answers

A–805

The Battle of Bull Run showed that both sides were unprepared and inexperienced and that the war would probably be long and hard.

A–806

The Anaconda Plan was a proposal by General Winfield Scott to choke the Confederacy by setting up a naval blockade and taking the Mississippi, thus cutting the South in two. They further captured a few strategic points in the South and waited for pro-Union southerners to overthrow the secessionists.

A–807

The blockade became increasingly successful in shutting out supplies from Europe.

Questions

Q–808

What were two reasons why many southerners believed that Great Britain and France would intervene on the Confederacy's behalf?

Your Answer _____

_____

Q–809

Where did Great Britain obtain cotton after the supply from the South was cut off?

Your Answer _____

_____

Q–810

How did the British public feel about slavery?

Your Answer _____

_____

Correct Answers

A–808

1) Great Britain and France would be happy to see a divided and weakened America.
2) British and French factories needed cotton.

A–809

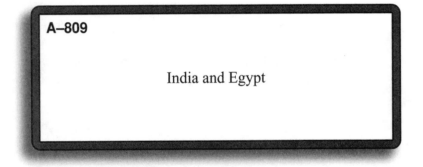

India and Egypt

A–810

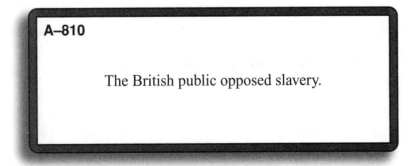

The British public opposed slavery.

Questions

Q–811

What product did Great Britain import from the North?

Your Answer _____

_____

Q–812

What was the *Trent* incident?

Your Answer _____

_____

Q–813

What were the names of the ironclads for the North and the South that fought to a stalemate in 1862?

Your Answer _____

_____

Correct Answers

A–811

Wheat

A–812

The North removed two Confederate envoys from the British ship *Trent*. The British considered it a violation of its rights on the high seas. The envoys were later released.

A–813

The USS *Monitor* and the CSS *Virginia*

Questions

Q–814

How did northerners and southerners show opposition to the draft?

Your Answer _____

Q–815

Why did prices in the South skyrocket?

Your Answer _____

Q–816

Why did many southern governors and other officials obstruct the actions of President Jefferson Davis?

Your Answer _____

Correct Answers

A–814

New Yorkers rioted while many southerners who were unable to hire a substitute avoided the draft or deserted the army after being drafted.

A–815

Goods were in short supply, and the South issued so much paper money that it became practically worthless.

A–816

They felt his actions violated states' rights.

Questions

Q–817

What did the Emancipation Proclamation do?

Your Answer _____

Q–818

Why did President Lincoln wait several months to issue the Emancipation Proclamation?

Your Answer _____

Q–819

What was the result of the Battle of Gettysburg?

Your Answer _____

Correct Answers

A–817

The Emancipation Proclamation freed all slaves in areas still in rebellion against the United States.

A–818

Lincoln did not want to make it appear an act of desperation after a series of northern defeats. So he waited until after the North "won" the Battle of Antietam.

A–819

General Robert E. Lee was defeated and was never again able to invade the North.

Questions

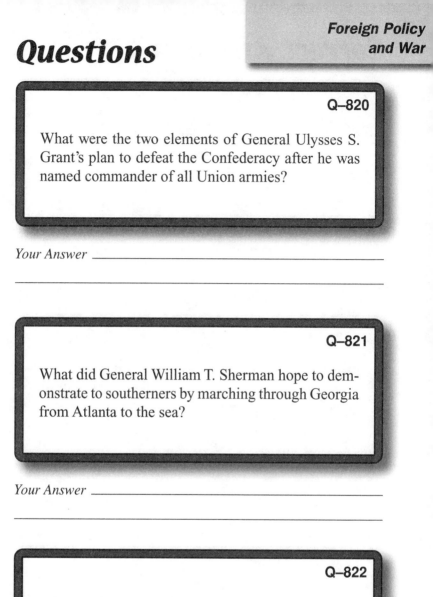

Q–820

What were the two elements of General Ulysses S. Grant's plan to defeat the Confederacy after he was named commander of all Union armies?

Your Answer _____

_____

Q–821

What did General William T. Sherman hope to demonstrate to southerners by marching through Georgia from Atlanta to the sea?

Your Answer _____

_____

Q–822

When and where did General Robert E. Lee surrender to General Ulysses S. Grant?

Your Answer _____

_____

Correct Answers

A–820

A drive by General William T. Sherman toward Atlanta, Georgia, and a drive by Grant and General George Gordon Meade toward Richmond, Virginia

A–821

Sherman wanted to impress on southerners that continuing the war could only mean ruin for all of them.

A–822

Lee surrendered on April 9, 1865, at Appomattox, Virginia.

Q–823

What European country tried to take over Mexico while the United States was involved in the Civil War?

Your Answer _____

Q–824

What did President Andrew Johnson do to persuade France to withdraw its troops from Mexico?

Your Answer _____

Q–825

What were the three main goals of the "new imperialism" of the 1870s?

Your Answer _____

Correct Answers

A–823

France

A–824

Johnson sent an American army to the Rio Grande and tacitly recognized the government of Benito Juarez.

A–825

1) Markets for surplus industrial production
2) Access to needed raw materials
3) Opportunities for overseas investment during a time of domestic economic depression

Questions

Q–826

What was the U.S. policy toward Korea in the 1880s?

Your Answer _____

_____

Q–827

What were the causes of the Sioux War?

Your Answer _____

_____

Q–828

What factors other than superior U.S. military force contributed to the defeat of the Native American tribes in the 1870s?

Your Answer _____

_____

Correct Answers

A–826

The United States promoted equal opportunity of trade and the sovereignty of Korea.

A–827

Westward expansion and the discovery of gold in South Dakota

A–828

Disease, alcoholism, railway construction, and the virtual extermination of the bison

Questions

Q–829

What happened to the Native American tribes after their defeat by U.S. military forces in the 1870s?

Your Answer _____

_____

Q–830

How did Congress respond to the British and German banning of meat imports from the United States during the 1880s?

Your Answer _____

_____

Q–831

How did U.S.-Hawaiian relations progress?

Your Answer _____

_____

Correct Answers

A–829

The Native Americans were forced to live on isolated reservations.

A–830

Congress set up a system of government regulation and inspection of meat for export.

A–831

In 1886, the United States obtained Pearl Harbor by signing a treaty with Hawaii. In 1893, pro-American sugar planters overthrew Queen Liliuokalani and the Hawaiian government. Finally, in 1898, Hawaii was annexed by the United States.

Questions

Q–832

Why did the Cuban revolt against Spain in 1895 affect the United States?

Your Answer _____

Q–833

What policy toward Cuba did Assistant Secretary of the Navy Theodore Roosevelt advocate?

Your Answer _____

Q–834

Why were Venezuela and the British colony of Guiana fighting?

Your Answer _____

555

Correct Answers

A–832

The United States was affected because Americans had money invested in Cuba and did considerable business there.

A–833

Direct military intervention by the United States

A–834

Both claimed an area in which gold had been discovered. The United States supported British claims in 1895 when Britain agreed to recognize the Monroe Doctrine in Latin America.

Questions

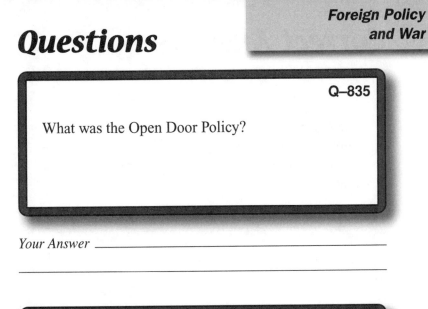

Q–835

What was the Open Door Policy?

Your Answer _____

Q–836

What was the DeLome letter?

Your Answer _____

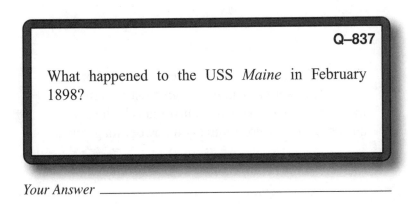

Q–837

What happened to the USS *Maine* in February 1898?

Your Answer _____

Correct Answers

A–835

The Open Door Policy was an American policy designed to protect China's political independence and promote equal opportunity of trade with that country.

A–836

The DeLome letter was written by the Spanish foreign minister in Washington criticizing President William McKinley in personally insulting terms.

A–837

The USS *Maine* blew up in Havana Harbor; 250 Americans were killed. Although most Americans at the time blamed Spain, most historians believe it was an accidental explosion in a gunpowder magazine.

Q–838

What caused most of the American casualties in Cuba?

Your Answer _____

_____

Q–839

What were the three main reasons for the American declaration of war against Spain?

Your Answer _____

_____

Q–840

What were the terms of President McKinley's ultimatum to Spain?

Your Answer _____

_____

Correct Answers

A–838

Disease and food poisoning

A–839

1) Loss of markets
2) Threats to Americans in Cuba
3) The inability of Spain and Cuba to resolve the Cuban revolution

A–840

An armistice in the fighting between Spain and Cuba, acceptance of American mediation to end the conflict, and an end to the Spanish use of concentration camps in Cuba

Questions

Q–841

What did Cuba and the United States gain as a result of the Treaty of Paris in 1898?

Your Answer _____

_____

Q–842

Who was Emilio Aguinaldo?

Your Answer _____

_____

Q–843

What was the Boxer Rebellion?

Your Answer _____

_____

Correct Answers

A–841

Cuba gained independence. The United States gained Guam, Puerto Rico, and the Philippines.

A–842

Emilio Aguinaldo was a Filipino nationalist who led a fight for independence against the United States.

A–843

The Boxer Rebellion was a revolt by Chinese nationalists against foreign settlements in China and against the Manchu government for granting industrial concessions in China to foreign nations.

Questions

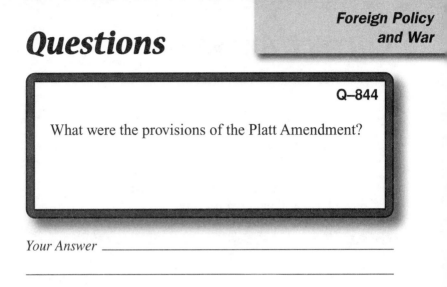

Q–844

What were the provisions of the Platt Amendment?

Your Answer _____

_____

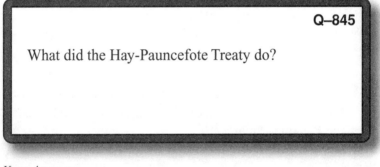

Q–845

What did the Hay-Pauncefote Treaty do?

Your Answer _____

_____

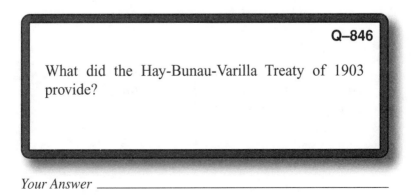

Q–846

What did the Hay-Bunau-Varilla Treaty of 1903 provide?

Your Answer _____

_____

Correct Answers

A–844

The Platt Amendment prohibited Cuba from running up too high a public debt and from making treaties that would impair its independence. The United States also received a ninety-nine-year lease of the naval base at Guantanamo Bay.

A–845

The Hay-Pauncefote Treaty abrogated an earlier agreement between the United States and Great Britain to jointly build a canal in Central America. It also opened the way for the United States to build the Panama Canal.

A–846

The Hay-Bunau-Varilla Treaty provided for U.S. control of the Panama Canal Zone for $10 million and an annual fee of $250,000.

Questions

Q–847

What was the Roosevelt Corollary to the Monroe Doctrine?

Your Answer _____

_____

Q–848

In which Latin American nations did the United States intervene during the early 1900s?

Your Answer _____

_____

Q–849

How did "dollar diplomacy" differ from "big stick" diplomacy?

Your Answer _____

_____

Correct Answers

A–847

The Roosevelt Corollary established the U.S. policy of intervening in the internal affairs of Latin American nations to keep European nations from using military force to collect debts.

A–848

Venezuela, Haiti, the Dominican Republic, Nicaragua, and Cuba

---

A–849

"Dollar diplomacy" emphasized economic development, while "big stick" diplomacy emphasized military and political intervention.

Questions

Q–850

What controversies surrounded the Treaty of Portsmouth in 1905?

Your Answer _____

_____

Q–851

What led to the Gentleman's Agreement? What did Japan and the United States agree to do?

Your Answer _____

_____

Q–852

What did President Theodore Roosevelt hope to accomplish by sending the great white naval fleet to Asian ports?

Your Answer _____

_____

Correct Answers

A–850

The Treaty of Portsmouth officially ended the Russo-Japanese War. Although Japan was the clear winner of the war, the Japanese did not feel that they received fair territorial and financial compensation from Russia. President Theodore Roosevelt was awarded a Nobel Peace Prize for helping to negotiate the treaty.

A–851

1) Numerous incidents of racial discrimination against Japanese had occurred in California.
2) Japan agreed to restrict the immigration of unskilled Japanese workers to the United States, and the United States agreed to end the segregation in California schools.

A–852

Roosevelt hoped to show American strength to China and Japan.

Questions

Q–853

Why did American troops invade Mexico in 1914?

Your Answer _____

_____

Q–854

What led Senator Henry Cabot Lodge to propose the Lodge Corollary to the Monroe Doctrine?

Your Answer _____

_____

Q–855

What countries constituted the Triple Entente and Triple Alliance?

Your Answer _____

_____

Correct Answers

A–853

General Victoriano Huerto rejected President Woodrow Wilson's call for democratic elections in Mexico and the establishment of a constitutional government.

A–854

A proposal by a Japanese syndicate to buy a large tract of land in Mexico's Lower California

A–855

The Triple Entente included Great Britain, France, and Russia. The Triple Alliance included Germany, Austria-Hungary, and Italy (although Italy did not join the Central Powers).

Questions

Q–856

What was the basic promise of President Wilson's "New Freedom" foreign policy?

Your Answer _____

_____

Q–857

What incident led Austria to interfere in Serbia in 1914?

Your Answer _____

_____

Q–858

What was the Submarine Crisis of 1915?

Your Answer _____

_____

Correct Answers

A–856

Wilson promised a more moral foreign policy, denounced imperialism and dollar diplomacy, and advocated the advancement of democratic capitalist governments throughout the world.

A–857

The assassination of the heir to the Austrian Hapsburg empire

A–858

The Germans sank the British liner *Lusitania* off the coast of Ireland on May 7, 1915, resulting in the loss of 1,198 lives, including 128 Americans. President Wilson had argued that Americans had a right as neutrals to travel safely on such ships, and he strongly protested the German action.

Questions

Q–859

What event precipitated the American military intervention in Mexico in 1916?

Your Answer _____

_____

Q–860

What was the Sussex Pledge?

Your Answer _____

_____

Q–861

How did World War I affect the 1916 presidential election?

Your Answer _____

_____

Correct Answers

A–859

Former Mexican general Francisco "Pancho" Villa shot sixteen Americans on a train in northern Mexico and burned the border town of Columbus, New Mexico. Villa was actually hoping to provoke American intervention as a means of undermining his political rival Venustiano Carranza.

A–860

The Germans pledged to give adequate warning before sinking merchant and passenger ships and to provide for the safety of passengers and crew. The Sussex Pledge was prompted by the torpedoing of the French passenger steamer, the *Sussex*, on March 24, 1916.

A–861

The slogan "He kept us out of the war" became the principal theme of Democratic campaign materials, and it apparently contributed to President Wilson's reelection.

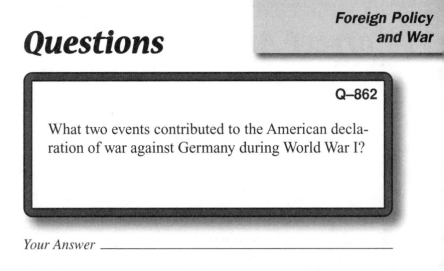

Q–862

What two events contributed to the American declaration of war against Germany during World War I?

Your Answer _____

_____

Q–863

When was the military draft enacted in World War I?

Your Answer _____

_____

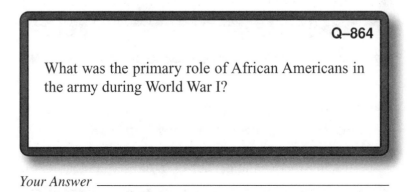

Q–864

What was the primary role of African Americans in the army during World War I?

Your Answer _____

_____

Correct Answers

A–862

1) Unlimited submarine warfare: Germany announced on January 31, 1917, that it would sink all ships, without warning, in a large war zone off the coasts of the Allied nations in the eastern Atlantic and Mediterranean.
2) The Zimmerman telegram: The British intercepted a secret message from the German foreign secretary, Arthur Zimmerman, to the German minister in Mexico in which the Germans proposed that, in the event of war between the United States and Germany, Mexico attack the United States. When the telegram was released to the press on March 1, 1917, many Americans became convinced that war with Germany was necessary.

A–863

The Selective Service Act was passed on May 18, 1917.

A–864

African Americans were kept in segregated units, usually with white officers, and were used as labor battalions or for other support activities. Some African American units, however, did see combat.

Questions

Q–865

What was the Fuel Administration?

Your Answer _____

_____

Q–866

What was the purpose of the War Industries Board?

Your Answer _____

_____

Q–867

What was the War Labor Board? How did World War I affect union membership?

Your Answer _____

_____

Correct Answers

A–865

Established in 1917, the Fuel Administration was concerned primarily with coal production and conservation because coal was the predominant fuel of the time.

A–866

The War Industries Board coordinated industrial mobilization by allocating raw materials, standardizing manufactured products, and instituting strict production and purchasing controls.

A–867

1) The War Labor Board was created in April 1918 to prevent strikes and work stoppages in war industries.
2) Union membership doubled during the war from about 2.5 million to 5 million.

Questions

Q–868

Describe the Espionage and Sedition Acts.

Your Answer _____

_____

Q–869

What was the American response when World War I broke out in Europe?

Your Answer _____

_____

Q–870

What happened to the United States as a result of World War I?

Your Answer _____

_____

Correct Answers

A–868

The Espionage Act of 1917 provided for fines and imprisonment for persons who made false statements that aided the enemy, incited rebellion in the military, or obstructed recruitment or the draft. The Sedition Act of May 1918 forbade any criticism of the government, flag, or uniform, even if there were not detrimental consequences.

A–869

President Wilson issued a proclamation of American neutrality on August 4, 1914.

A–870

The United States emerged as the economic and political leader of the world.

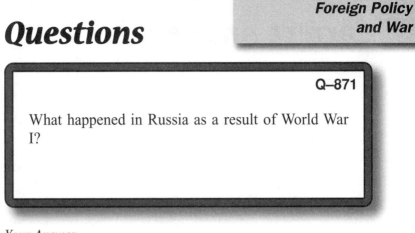

Q–871

What happened in Russia as a result of World War I?

Your Answer _____

_____

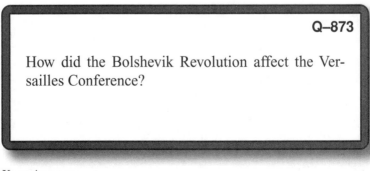

Q–872

What was the name of President Wilson's peace plan? What was its primary message?

Your Answer _____

_____

Q–873

How did the Bolshevik Revolution affect the Versailles Conference?

Your Answer _____

_____

Correct Answers

A–871

The tsar was overthrown and a Communist dictatorship was set up.

A–872

1) Wilson's plan was called the Fourteen Points.
2) Its primary message was that there should be peace without victory, meaning that the victors should not be vindictive toward the losers.

A–873

The threat of international communism resulted in the Western powers remaining united after the war.

Questions

Q–874

What was President Wilson's biggest mistake concerning the Paris Peace Conference?

Your Answer _____

_____

Q–875

Name four important provisions of the Versailles Treaty.

Your Answer _____

_____

Q–876

What was the main objection Republicans had to the League of Nations? How did the Senate vote on the League of Nations?

Your Answer _____

_____

Correct Answers

A–874

Wilson did not appoint any Republican to the American delegation and did not consult Republican leadership in the Senate about the negotiations. Consequently, Wilson did not receive bipartisan support for his efforts at the conference.

A–875

1) The League of Nations was formed.
2) Germany was held responsible for causing the war. This decision was clearly contrary to the idea of peace without victory.
3) The new nations of eastern and central Europe partially fulfilled the idea of self-determination for all nationalities, but the boundaries drawn at the conference left many people under the control of other nationalities.
4) German colonies were made mandates of the League of Nations and given in trusteeship to France, Japan, and Britain.

A–876

1) Republicans feared that Article X of the League Covenant would force the United States to go to war without the approval of Congress.
2) On November 19, 1919, the treaty failed to get enough votes. This was also due to President Wilson's uncompromising position.

Questions

Q–877

What was the effect of the Versailles Conference on Germany?

Your Answer _____

_____

Q–878

Name the three treaties that resulted from the Washington Conference. Briefly describe each treaty.

Your Answer _____

_____

Q–879

What did the Dawes Plan do?

Your Answer _____

_____

Correct Answers

A–877

The Versailles Conference created bitterness and a desire for revenge among the German people, which led to the rise of Adolf Hitler and the Nazi movement.

A–878

1) Five-Power Pact: Ended new construction of capital naval vessels
2) Nine-Power Pact: Upheld the open door in China
3) Four-Power Pact: Bound the United States, Great Britain, Japan, and France to respect each other's possessions in the Pacific

A–879

The Dawes Plan helped Germany, which was bankrupt, pay reparations to the Allies by having American banks make loans of $2.5 billion to Germany by 1930.

Questions

Q–880

What was the Kellogg-Briand Pact? What was its major flaw?

Your Answer _____

Q–881

What did the Indian Reorganization Act of 1934 do?

Your Answer _____

Q–882

What was the Good Neighbor Policy?

Your Answer _____

Correct Answers

A–880

1) The Kellogg-Briand Pact was a treaty signed at Paris in August 1928 that renounced war as an instrument of national policy.
2) The treaty had no enforcement provisions.

A–881

The Indian Reorganization Act restored tribal ownership of lands, recognized tribal constitutions and government, and provided loans to tribes for economic development.

A–882

The Good Neighbor Policy was an attempt by President Franklin D. Roosevelt's administration to improve relations with Latin American nations.

Questions

Q–883

What did the Neutrality Acts of 1935, 1936, 1937, and 1939 do?

Your Answer _____

_____

Q–884

What treaty did Germany defy when it occupied the Rhineland in 1936?

Your Answer _____

_____

Q–885

In what years did the following events occur?
1) Formation of the Rome-Berlin Axis
2) Japanese invasion of China
3) Union of Germany and Austria
4) German occupation of all of Czechoslovakia

Your Answer _____

_____

Correct Answers

A–883

1) 1935: Tried to maintain U.S. neutrality and isolation
2) 1936: Prohibited any loans or credits to belligerents
3) 1937: Allowed for cash and carry of nonmilitary goods to belligerents
4) 1939: Allowed for cash and carry of arms to belligerents, but forbade American shipping to trade with belligerents or Americans to be on belligerent ships

A–884

The Versailles Treaty

A–885

1) 1936
2) 1937
3) 1938
4) 1939

Questions

Q–886

How did the United States respond to Japan gaining military control of southern Indochina from Vichy France?

Your Answer _____

Q–887

In what year was the War Resources Board created and what was its purpose?

Your Answer _____

Q–888

What was the Greater East Asia Co-Prosperity sphere?

Your Answer _____

Correct Answers

A–886

The United States responded by freezing Japanese funds in the United States, closing the Panama Canal to Japan, activating the Philippine Militia, and placing an embargo on the export of oil and other vital products to Japan.

A–887

The War Resources Board was created in 1939 by President Franklin Roosevelt to develop a plan for industrial mobilization in the event of war.

A–888

The Greater East Asia Co-Prosperity sphere was the Japanese term for their goal of an empire of undefined boundaries in east Asia and the western Pacific.

Questions

Q–889

What did the 1940 embargo against Japan involve?

Your Answer _____

Q–890

What was the aim of the America First Committee?

Your Answer _____

Q–891

What was the Atlantic Charter?

Your Answer _____

Correct Answers

A–889

The embargo involved the export of aviator gasoline, lubricants, and scrap iron. In December 1940, the embargo was extended to include iron ore and pig iron, some chemicals, and machine tools.

A–890

To keep America out of World War II

A–891

The Atlantic Charter was a statement of principles issued by President Franklin Roosevelt and British Prime Minister Winston Churchill that described a postwar world based on self-determination for all nations. It also endorsed the principles of freedom of speech and religion and freedom from want and fear.

Questions

Q–892

How did the United States respond to the German invasion of the Soviet Union?

Your Answer _____

_____

Q–893

When was the Lend-Lease Act passed? What did it provide for? What was its significance?

Your Answer _____

_____

Q–894

How did President Franklin Roosevelt describe the December 7, 1941, Japanese attack on Pearl Harbor?

Your Answer _____

_____

Correct Answers

A–892

The United States extended Lend-Lease assistance to the Soviet Union.

A–893

1) March 1941
2) The Lend-Lease Act made available $7 million for war materials that President Franklin Roosevelt could sell, lend, lease, exchange, or transfer to any country whose defense he deemed vital to the United States.
3) It indicated that the United States was moving toward stronger support for Britain.

A–894

"A date which will live in infamy"

Questions

Q–895

When was the War Production Board established? What was its purpose?

Your Answer _____

_____

Q–896

When was the Casablanca Conference? What was its significance?

Your Answer _____

_____

Q–897

When was the Declaration of Cairo issued? What did it call for?

Your Answer _____

_____

Correct Answers

A–895

1) 1942
2) To regulate the use of raw materials

A–896

1) January 14 to 25, 1943
2) During this conference, President Franklin Roosevelt and Prime Minister Churchill declared a policy of unconditional surrender for "all enemies."

A–897

1) December 1, 1943
2) The Declaration of Cairo called for Japan's unconditional surrender and stated that all Chinese territories occupied by Japan would be returned to China and that Korea would be free and independent.

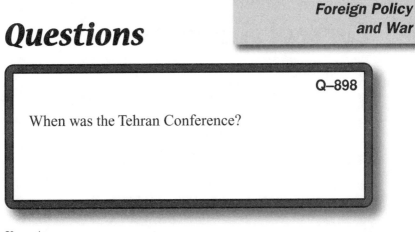

Q–898

When was the Tehran Conference?

Your Answer _____

_____

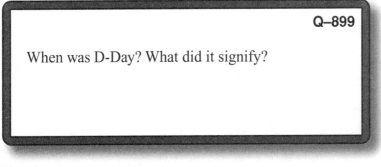

Q–899

When was D-Day? What did it signify?

Your Answer _____

_____

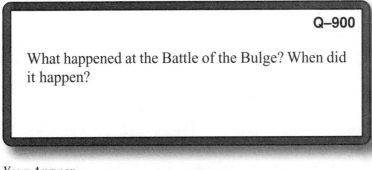

Q–900

What happened at the Battle of the Bulge? When did it happen?

Your Answer _____

_____

Correct Answers

A–898

November 28 to December 1, 1943

A–899

1) June 6, 1944
2) D-Day signified the beginning of the liberation of Europe by the Allied forces.

A–900

1) At the Battle of the Bulge, the Germans counter-attacked, driving the Allies back about fifty miles into Belgium.
2) It began on December 16, 1944. By January, however, the Allies were once more advancing toward Germany.

Questions

Q–901

What was the Battle of the Coral Sea? What was its significance?

Your Answer _____

_____

Q–902

What happened at the Battle of Midway? Why was it important?

Your Answer _____

_____

Q–903

What was the significance of the Battle of Okinawa?

Your Answer _____

_____

Correct Answers

A–901

1) The Battle of the Coral Sea occurred May 7 to 8, 1942. Planes from the American carriers *Lexington* and *Yorktown* forced Japanese troop transports to turn back from attacking Port Moresby.
2) The battle stopped the Japanese advance on Australia.

A–902

1) At the Battle of Midway, American air power destroyed four Japanese carriers and about 300 planes.
2) The battle proved to be the turning point in the Pacific War.

A–903

The Battle of Okinawa virtually destroyed Japan's remaining defenses.

Questions

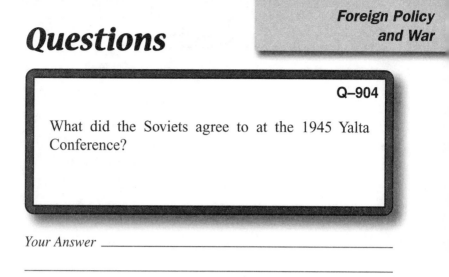

Q–904

What did the Soviets agree to at the 1945 Yalta Conference?

Your Answer _____

_____

Q–905

When did Germany surrender?

Your Answer _____

_____

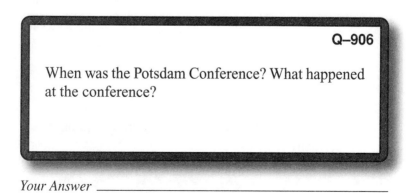

Q–906

When was the Potsdam Conference? What happened at the conference?

Your Answer _____

_____

Correct Answers

A–904

The Soviets agreed to enter the Pacific War within three months after Germany surrendered and agreed to the "Declaration of Liberated Europe," which called for free elections.

A–905

May 7, 1945

A–906

1) July 17 to August 2, 1945
2) The United States, Great Britain, and the Soviet Union agreed to the concept of war crimes trials and the demilitarization and denazification of Germany.

Questions

Q–907

When did Japan announce its surrender?

Your Answer _____

_____

Q–908

When was the United Nations formed? What countries
are permanent members of the Security Council?

Your Answer _____

_____

Q–909

What famous speech was given in Fulton, Missouri,
in 1946?

Your Answer _____

_____

Correct Answers

A–907

August 14, 1945

A–908

1) The United Nations was formed in 1945.
2) The United States, Great Britain, France, Russia (formerly the Soviet Union), and China are all permanent members.

A–909

Winston Churchill's "Iron Curtain" speech, in which he stated that an Iron Curtain had spread across Europe separating the democratic West from the Communist East

Questions

Q–910

What was the name of the United States' policy toward the Soviet Union in the postwar era?

Your Answer _____

Q–911

What was the Truman Doctrine? In what two countries was it first invoked?

Your Answer _____

Q–912

What was the objective of the Marshall Plan?

Your Answer _____

Correct Answers

A–910

Containment

A–911

1) The Truman Doctrine stated that the United States must support free peoples who were existing under Communist domination.
2) The doctrine was first invoked when the United States gave military and economic aid to Greece and Turkey in 1947.

A–912

The Marshall Plan provided economic aid to help rebuild postwar Europe as a means of preventing Communist expansion.

Questions

Q–913

What Soviet action prompted the Berlin Crisis in June 1948? How did the United States respond?

Your Answer _____

Q–914

When was the North Atlantic Treaty Organization (NATO) formed? What did all of its members pledge?

Your Answer _____

Q–915

Who headed the Allied Control Council that governed Japan after the war?

Your Answer _____

Correct Answers

A–913

1) The Soviets blocked surface access to Berlin.
2) The United States instituted an airlift to transport supplies to the city until the Soviets lifted their blockade in May 1949.

A–914

1) April 1949
2) That an attack against one would be considered an attack against all

A–915

General Douglas MacArthur

Questions

Q–916

When did the Communists take over China? Who was the leader of the Communist forces?

Your Answer _____

_____

Q–917

Why did President Harry Truman remove General Douglas MacArthur from his command during the Korean War?

Your Answer _____

_____

Q–918

When was the Korean armistice signed? What was the war's outcome?

Your Answer _____

_____

Correct Answers

A–916

1) 1949
2) Mao Tse-tung

A–917

Because McArthur criticized the president for fighting a limited war. MacArthur called for a naval blockade of China and bombing north of the Yalu River.

A–918

1) June 1953
2) Korea was divided along virtually the same boundary that had existed prior to the war.

Q–919

Who became the new Soviet leader after Joseph Stalin died in 1953?

Your Answer _____

_____

Q–920

When was the Southeast Asia Treaty Organization formed? What Asian countries joined?

Your Answer _____

_____

Q–921

What happened to Vietnam as a result of the Geneva Accords? What role did the United States play after the accords were signed?

Your Answer _____

_____

Correct Answers

A–919

Nikita Khrushchev

A–920

1) September 1954
2) Philippines, Thailand, and Pakistan

A–921

1) Vietnam was split along the 17th parallel into North and South Vietnam.
2) The United States supplied aid to South Vietnam.

Questions

Q–922

When was the Suez Canal crisis? What was its significance?

Your Answer _____

_____

Q–923

What was the Eisenhower Doctrine?

Your Answer _____

_____

Q–924

What was the U-2 incident?

Your Answer _____

_____

Correct Answers

A–922

1) 1956
2) The United States refused to support its allies France, Great Britain, and Israel when they attacked Egypt after Egyptian President Gamal Abdel Nasser nationalized the canal.

A–923

The Eisenhower Doctrine was a pledge made by President Dwight D. Eisenhower in January 1957 that the United States was prepared to use armed force in the Middle East against Communist aggression.

A–924

On May 1, 1960, an American U-2 spy plane was shot down over the Soviet Union. President Eisenhower took responsibility for the spy plane, and Soviet leader Nikita Khrushchev angrily called off the Paris summit conference that was to take place in a few days.

Questions

Q–925

Why did the United States support the overthrow of President Jacobo Arbenz Guzman of Guatemala in 1954?

Your Answer _____

_____

Q–926

What was the Bay of Pigs operation?

Your Answer _____

_____

Q–927

What did the Alliance for Progress provide? When was it founded?

Your Answer _____

_____

Correct Answers

A–925

Guzman had begun accepting arms from the Soviet Union.

A–926

Under President Eisenhower, the CIA trained some 2,000 men for an invasion of Cuba to overthrow Fidel Castro. On April 19, 1961, during John F. Kennedy's administration, this force invaded Cuba at the Bay of Pigs but was pinned down and forced to surrender.

A–927

1) The Alliance for Progress provided $20 million in aid for Latin America.
2) 1961

Questions

Q–928

How did President John F. Kennedy respond to the building of Soviet missile sites in Cuba? What year did this happen? How was it resolved?

Your Answer _____

_____

Q–929

When was the Peace Corps established? What was its purpose?

Your Answer _____

_____

Q–930

What prompted the Gulf of Tonkin Resolution in 1964? What did the resolution do?

Your Answer _____

_____

Correct Answers

A–928

1) Kennedy announced a blockade of Cuba and called on Soviet leader Nikita Khrushchev to dismantle the missile base.
2) 1962
3) Khrushchev backed down and withdrew the missiles.

A–929

1) 1961
2) The Peace Corps sent young volunteers to third-world countries to contribute their skills in locally sponsored projects.

A–930

1) The Gulf of Tonkin Resolution was prompted by an alleged attack by North Vietnamese gunboats on American destroyers.
2) The resolution authorized President Lyndon Johnson to use military force in Vietnam.

Questions

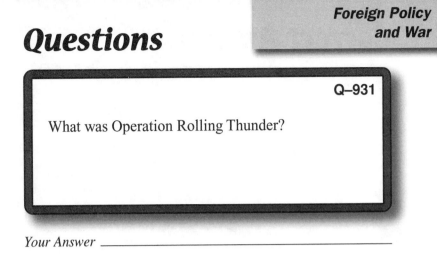

Q–931

What was Operation Rolling Thunder?

Your Answer _____

_____

Q–932

What was the "Domino Theory"?

Your Answer _____

_____

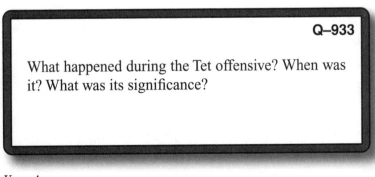

Q–933

What happened during the Tet offensive? When was it? What was its significance?

Your Answer _____

_____

Correct Answers

A–931

The first sustained American bombing of North Vietnam

A–932

The Domino Theory justified American involvement in Vietnam by arguing that if Vietnam fell to the Communists, all of Southeast Asia would eventually fall as well.

A–933

1) The Vietcong attacked numerous South Vietnamese cities and towns, American bases, and Saigon.
2) January 1968
3) Although they suffered large losses, the Vietcong won a psychological victory as American opinion began turning against the war.

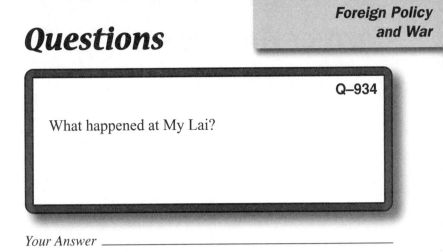

Q–934

What happened at My Lai?

Your Answer _____

_____

Q–935

What was "Vietnamization"?

Your Answer _____

_____

Q–936

What were the Pentagon Papers?

Your Answer _____

_____

Correct Answers

A–934

An American massacre of the Vietnamese

A–935

"Vietnamization" was President Richard Nixon's policy of building up South Vietnamese forces while gradually withdrawing American troops.

A–936

The Pentagon Papers were classified Defense Department documents published in 1971, against the protests of the Nixon administration, which revealed that the government had misled the Congress and the American people regarding its intentions in Vietnam during the mid-1960s.

Questions

Q–937

What were the three key elements of the peace treaty negotiated in 1972 between the United States and North Vietnam?

Your Answer —————————————————————

—————————————————————————————

Q–938

What bold diplomatic initiatives did President Nixon begin in 1972?

Your Answer —————————————————————

—————————————————————————————

Q–939

What was the SALT of 1972?

Your Answer —————————————————————

—————————————————————————————

Correct Answers

A–937

1) A cease-fire
2) Return of American prisoners of war
3) Withdrawal of U.S. forces from Vietnam

A–938

Nixon sent National Security Advisor Henry Kissinger on secret missions to plan summit meetings in both China and the Soviet Union.

A–939

The Strategic Arms Limitation Treaty (SALT) was a treaty signed by the United States and the Soviet Union in 1972 in which both sides agreed to stop making ballistic missiles and to reduce the number of antiballistic missiles to 200 for each power.

Questions

Q–940

What was "détente"?

Your Answer _____

Q–941

What is OPEC? How did it affect the United States in the 1970s?

Your Answer _____

Q–942

When did the last U.S. combat troops leave Vietnam? When did Saigon fall?

Your Answer _____

Correct Answers

A–940

A policy initiated during the Nixon administration that aimed to reduce the amount of tension between the United States and the Soviet Union

A–941

1) The Organization of Petroleum Exporting Countries (OPEC) is a cartel of oil-producing nations; its founding members are Venezuela, Saudi Arabia, Kuwait, Iraq, and Iran.
2) OPEC significantly raised oil prices in the early 1970s. This action doubled gas prices in the United States and raised inflation above 10 percent.

A–942

1) U.S. troops left by 1973.
2) Saigon fell in 1975.

Questions

Q–943

What was the basis of President Jimmy Carter's foreign policy?

Your Answer _____

_____

Q–944

When was the Panama Canal Treaty negotiated? What did it provide?

Your Answer _____

_____

Q–945

What were the major provisions of the 1978 Camp David Accords?

Your Answer _____

_____

Correct Answers

A–943

Human rights considerations

A–944

1) 1978
2) The Panama Canal Treaty provided for the transfer of ownership of the canal to Panama in 1999 and guaranteed its neutrality.

A–945

Israel promised to return occupied land in the Sinai to Egypt in exchange for Egyptian recognition.

Questions

Q–946

How did the United States respond to the Soviet invasion of Afghanistan?

Your Answer _____

_____

Q–947

Why did Iranian "students" take over the U.S. Embassy in November 1979?

Your Answer _____

_____

Q–948

What was President Ronald Reagan's term to describe the Soviet Union?

Your Answer _____

_____

Correct Answers

A–946

The Carter administration stopped shipments of grain to the Soviet Union, withdrew SALT II from the Senate, and withdrew the United States from the 1980 Moscow Olympics.

A–947

The U.S. government had allowed the exiled shah of Iran to come to the United States for medical treatment, and the Iranians demanded that the shah be returned to Iran for trial. The United States refused the request.

A–948

The Evil Empire

Questions

Q–949

What two important events happened on January 20, 1981?

Your Answer _____

_____

Q–950

What was the Iran-Contra scandal all about?

Your Answer _____

_____

Q–951

Who became the new Soviet premier in March 1985? What were the characteristics of the new regime?

Your Answer _____

_____

Correct Answers

A–949

President Reagan was inaugurated, and American hostages were released from Iran.

A–950

It was revealed that the United States had sold arms to Iranians in hopes of encouraging them to use their influence to get American hostages in Lebanon released. The profits from these sales were then diverted to the Nicaraguan contras in an attempt to circumvent congressional restrictions on funding these countries.

A–951

1) Mikhail Gorbachev
2) A more flexible approach toward both domestic and foreign affairs

Q–952

What was SDI? What was its fate?

Your Answer _____

_____

Q–953

What was the justification for the United States invasion of Panama in 1989?

Your Answer _____

_____

Q–954

What was the first Eastern European country to shift away from communism in 1989?

Your Answer _____

_____

Correct Answers

A–952

1) The Strategic Defense Initiative (SDI) was a computer-controlled defense system, popularly called Star Wars, that would destroy enemy missiles from outer space.
2) Congress balked, skeptical about the technological possibilities and fearing enormous costs.

A–953

The alleged involvement of Panamanian dictator Manuel Noriega in the drug traffic between South America and the United States

A–954

Poland

Q–955

What event symbolized the collapse of communism in Eastern Europe?

Your Answer _____

_____

Q–956

How did the George H. W. Bush administration respond to the reduced threat from the Soviet Union?

Your Answer _____

_____

Q–957

What did the START I and II accomplish?

Your Answer _____

_____

Correct Answers

A–955

The fall of the Berlin Wall in 1989

A–956

In 1990, the Bush administration proposed to cut military spending by 10 percent and the armed forces by 25 percent.

A–957

Both Strategic Arms Reduction Treaties (START) reduced the number of nuclear warheads for the United States and Soviet Union (with START I reducing arsenals by approximately 30 percent).

Questions

Q–958

How did the United States respond to Iraq's invasion of Kuwait?

Your Answer _____

Q–959

What were the four terms for a cease-fire in the Gulf War established by the United Nations?

Your Answer _____

Q–960

When did the Communists lose their monopoly on political power in the Soviet Union? What event symbolized this change?

Your Answer _____

Correct Answers

A–958

The United States first sent 100,000 troops to Saudi Arabia as part of Operation Desert Shield. The United States then increased troop levels to 400,000 and set a January 15, 1991, deadline for Iraqi withdrawal from Kuwait. Operation Desert Storm (the First Gulf War) began on January 17, 1991.

A–959

1) Iraq had to rescind its annexation of Kuwait.
2) Iraq had to accept liability for damages and return Kuwaiti property.
3) Iraq had to end all military actions.
4) Iraq had to release all captives.

A–960

1) March 13, 1991
2) A decree allowing non-Communists to run for political office

Questions

Q–961

What were the three United States postwar goals for the Middle East? At what conference were these goals announced?

Your Answer

Q–962

When did the Soviet Union officially disband? What was it replaced by?

Your Answer

Q–963

What was the result of the 1994 accord signed between Israel and the Palestine Liberation Organization?

Your Answer

Correct Answers

A–961

1) Regional arms control and security arrangements; international aid for reconstruction of Iraq and Kuwait; and the resolution of the Israeli-Palestinian conflict
2) Middle East Conference held in Madrid, Spain, in October 1991

A–962

1) December 1991
2) The Commonwealth of Independent States

A–963

The accord established Palestinian self-rule in the Gaza Strip at Jericho.

Questions

Q–964

What was involved in the 1994 agreement between the United States and North Korea?

Your Answer _____

Q–965

Why did the Clinton administration lift the trade embargo against Vietnam in 1994?

Your Answer _____

Q–966

Describe the 1994 immigration agreement between the United States and Cuba.

Your Answer _____

Correct Answers

A–964

The United States would provide financial and technological assistance for North Korean nuclear energy in return for North Korea's accepting the Nuclear Non-Proliferation Treaty.

A–965

Because Vietnam cooperated with efforts to find the remains of U.S. military personnel, and U.S. businesses wanted to gain access to the Vietnamese market

A–966

The United States agreed to allow 20,000 Cubans into the country annually in return for the Cuban government preventing its citizens from leaving Cuba in rafts and other boats for illegal entry into the United States.

Q–967

Why was there strong opposition to the Clinton administration's decision to continue China's "most favored nation" trading status?

Your Answer _____

Legal Decisions

Q–968

What was the importance of the John Peter Zenger trial in 1735?

Your Answer _____

Q–969

What were writs of assistance and why were they issued?

Your Answer _____

Correct Answers

A–967

Because of the lack of improvements in political freedom in that country

A–968

Zenger was put on trial for allegedly printing libelous material about the governor of New York. Zenger's attorney successfully argued that Zenger's accusations were not libelous but were based in fact. Zenger was acquitted and the idea of freedom of the press was strengthened.

A–969

Writs of Assistance were general search warrants issued to help royal officials stop the evasion of British mercantilistic trade restrictions.

Questions

Q–970

What precedent was set by Chief Justice John Marshall in *Marbury v. Madison?*

Your Answer _____

_____

Q–971

How did Chief Justice Marshall's decisions affect the balance of powers between the federal and state governments?

Your Answer _____

_____

Q–972

What was the Supreme Court's decision in *Fletcher v. Peck?*

Your Answer _____

_____

Correct Answers

A–970

Marshall asserted the power of judicial review over federal legislation.

A–971

Marshall's decisions strengthened the federal and weakened the states' powers.

A–972

The Court decided that a Georgia state law was void because it violated a principle of the Constitution.

Questions

Q–973

What precedent was set in the *Dartmouth College v. Woodward* decision of 1819?

Your Answer _____

Q–974

Chief Justice Marshall ruled that no state has the right to control an agency of the federal government in the _____ v. _____ case of 1819.

Your Answer _____

Q–975

True or False: Chief Justice Marshall ruled that only Congress had the right to regulate commerce among states in *Gibbons v. Ogden* in 1824.

Your Answer _____

Correct Answers

A–973

The decision severely limited the power of the state governments to control corporations.

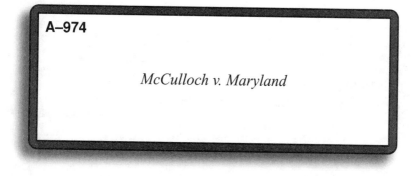

A–974

McCulloch v. Maryland

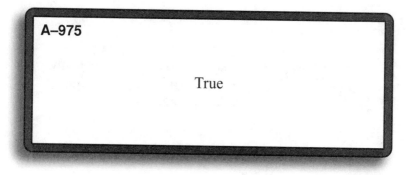

A–975

True

Questions

Q–976

What did the Supreme Court decide in *Worcester v. Georgia*?

Your Answer _____

Q–977

How did President Andrew Jackson react to the *Worcester v. Georgia* Supreme Court decision?

Your Answer _____

Q–978

What was the ruling in the Charles River Bridge case of 1837?

Your Answer _____

Correct Answers

A–976

The Supreme Court decision supported the claims of the Cherokee nation as being a sovereign entity within that state.

A–977

Jackson refused to enforce the court's decision.

A–978

The Court decided that a state could revoke a grant of monopoly if the original grant had ceased to be in the best interests of the community.

Questions

Q–979

How did the director of the National Bank, Nicholas Biddle, react to President Jackson's removal of federal money from his bank?

Your Answer _____

_____

Q–980

What were the effects of the Dred Scott decision?

Your Answer _____

_____

Q–981

What did the Supreme Court rule in the 1886 *Wabash* case?

Your Answer _____

_____

Correct Answers

A–979

Biddle tightened up credit and called in loans, which resulted in a financial recession.

A–980

Many southerners were encouraged to take an extreme position on the slavery issue and to refuse any compromise. Many northerners were convinced that the decision was not final and that a pro-slavery conspiracy controlled the government.

A–981

The Court ruled that only Congress, and not individual states, had the right to regulate interstate commerce and thus the railway industry.

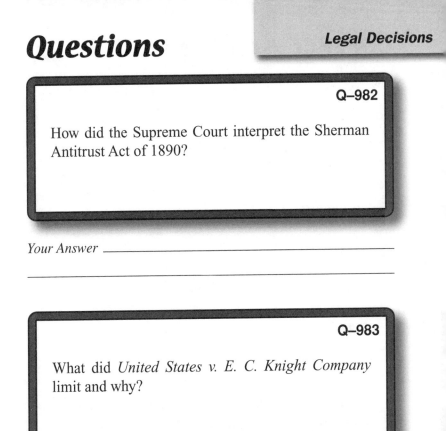

Q–982

How did the Supreme Court interpret the Sherman Antitrust Act of 1890?

Your Answer _____

Q–983

What did *United States v. E. C. Knight Company* limit and why?

Your Answer _____

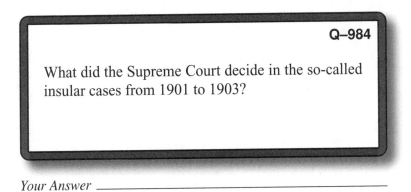

Q–984

What did the Supreme Court decide in the so-called insular cases from 1901 to 1903?

Your Answer _____

Correct Answers

A–982

The Court emphasized prosecutions against labor unions and farmers' cooperatives rather than against business trusts.

A–983

The decision limited the federal government's ability to regulate monopolies. Although the federal government could regulate the distribution of goods, the Supreme Court ruled that the federal government could not limit production in a state.

A–984

The Court decided that inhabitants of American territorial possessions did not have the constitutional rights of American citizens.

Questions

Q–985

What was the importance of the *Northern Securities Company v. United States* ruling?

Your Answer _____

_____

Q–986

What did the cases *Lochner v. New York* and *Muller v. Oregon* decide?

Your Answer _____

_____

Q–987

What policies regarding money did farm groups advocate during the 1870s and 1880s?

Your Answer _____

_____

Correct Answers

A–985

The U.S. government used the Sherman Antitrust Act to sue the Northern Securities Company for monopolistic activity. The U.S. government won the case and broke apart the Northern Securities Company. This was the first major "trust bust."

A–986

In *Lochner v. New York*, the Supreme Court ruled that laws limiting hours for bakers were unconstitutional since baking was not a hazardous profession. However, in *Muller v. Oregon*, the Court upheld laws limiting work hours for women because the Supreme Court ruled women were essential for reproduction and thus should be protected.

A–987

Currency inflation and the use of both gold and silver to back money

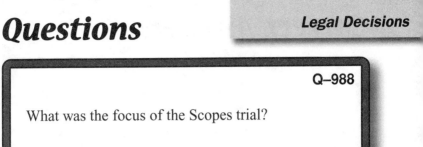

Q–988

What was the focus of the Scopes trial?

Your Answer _____

_____

Q–989

What Supreme Court decision upheld President Franklin Roosevelt's 1942 order that Japanese Americans be relocated to concentration camps? What year was the decision made? When were the camps closed?

Your Answer _____

_____

Q–990

What was the importance of the 1944 Supreme Court decision *Smith v. Millwright*?

Your Answer _____

_____

Correct Answers

A–988

The focus of the Scopes trial was whether evolution should be taught in the public schools. Although the defendant, a high school biology teacher named John Thomas Scopes, was convicted of violating a Tennessee law that forbade the teaching of evolution, the trial was largely seen as a victory for free speech.

A–989

1) *Korematsu v. United States*
2) 1944
3) March 1946

A–990

The *Smith v. Millwright* decision struck down the Texas primary elections, which were restricted to whites, for violating the Fifteenth Amendment.

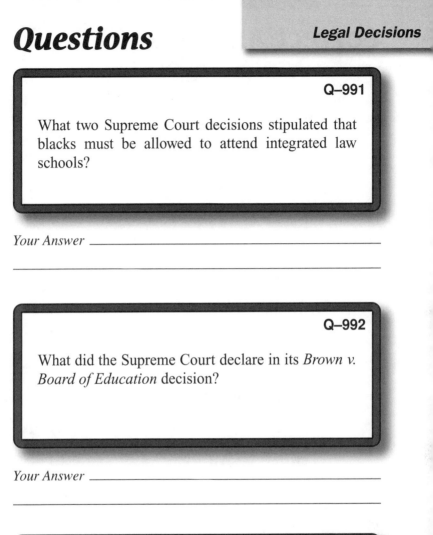

Q–991

What two Supreme Court decisions stipulated that blacks must be allowed to attend integrated law schools?

Your Answer _____

_____

Q–992

What did the Supreme Court declare in its *Brown v. Board of Education* decision?

Your Answer _____

_____

Q–993

What was the decision in *Engel v. Vitale*?

Your Answer _____

_____

Correct Answers

A–991

Ada Lois Sipuel v. Board of Regents (1948) and *Sweatt v. Painter* (1950)

A–992

In 1954, the Court declared that separate educational facilities were inherently unequal and that states had to integrate with "all deliberate speed."

A–993

The Supreme Court ruled that it was unconstitutional for public schools to compose and sponsor prayer.

Questions

Q–994

What did *Baker v. Carr* address?

Your Answer —————————————————

Q–995

What act of Congress did the *Heart of Atlanta Motel v. United States* strengthen?

Your Answer —————————————————

Q–996

What issue did *Furman v. Georgia* address?

Your Answer —————————————————

Correct Answers

A–994

The reapportionment of state legislatures so that each member represented the same number of constituents

A–995

The Civil Rights Act of 1964

A–996

The death penalty

Questions

Q–997

What did the Supreme Court decide in its 1973 *Roe v. Wade* decision?

Your Answer _____

Q–998

What First-Amendment right was tested in *New York Times Company v. United States*?

Your Answer _____

Q–999

Although *Bakke v. Regents of the University of California* maintained that affirmative action was constitutional, it declared that the use of _____ was not.

Your Answer _____

Correct Answers

A–997

Roe v. Wade legalized abortion during the first three months of pregnancy.

A–998

Whether the First-Amendment right to freedom of the press outweighed the federal executive branch's need to maintain secrecy

A–999

quotas

Questions

Q–1000

What 1989 Supreme Court decision shifted the focus of the abortion debate from the courts to the state legislatures?

Your Answer _____

_____

Correct Answers

A–1000

Webster v. Reproductive Health Services, in which the Supreme Court upheld a Missouri law prohibiting public employees from performing abortions unless the mother's life was threatened

STOP **Take Test-Readiness Quiz 4 on CD**
(to review questions 697-1000)

Blank Cards for
Your Own Questions

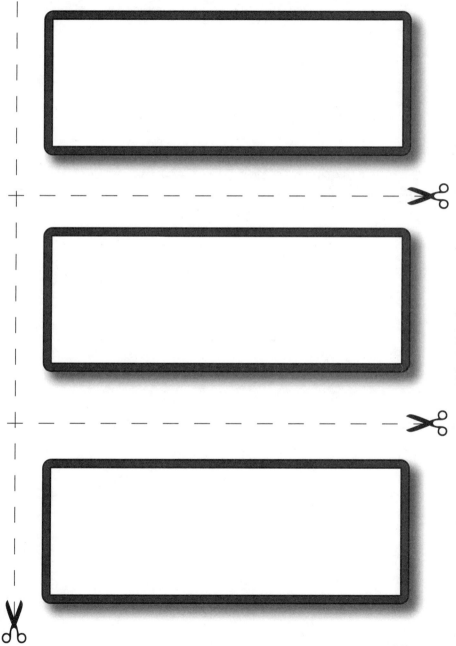

Correct Answers

Blank Cards for *Your Own Questions*

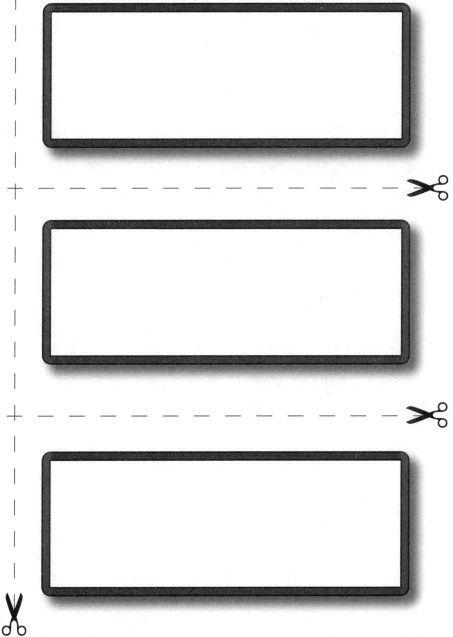

Correct Answers

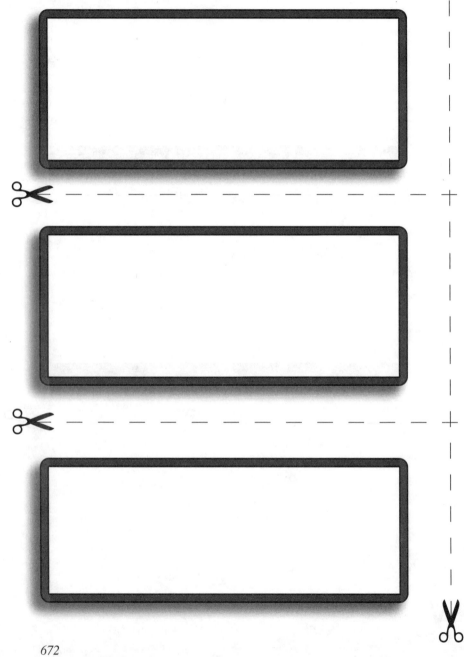

Blank Cards for *Your Own Questions*

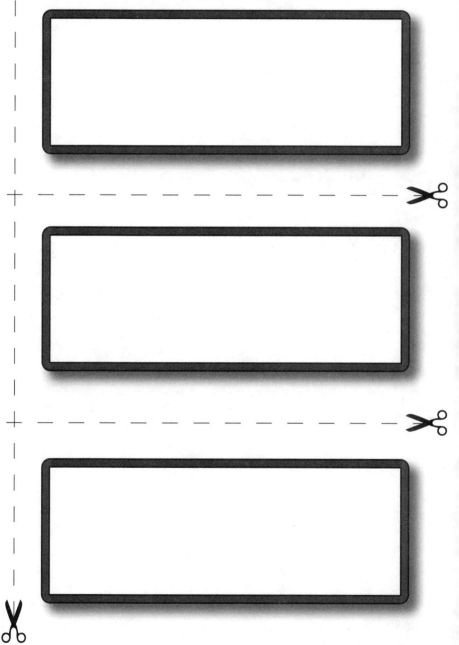

Correct Answers

Blank Cards for
Your Own Questions

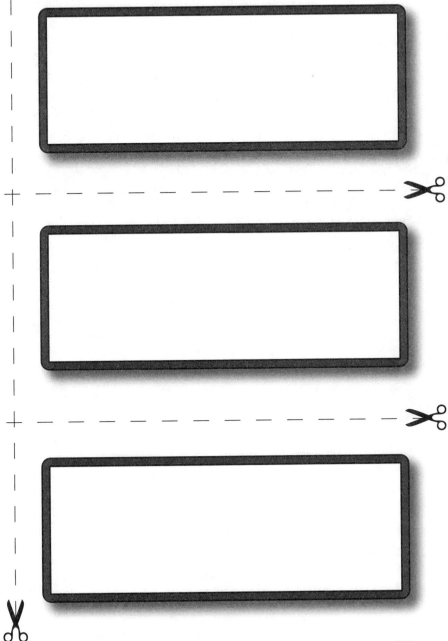

Correct Answers

Blank Cards for
Your Own Questions

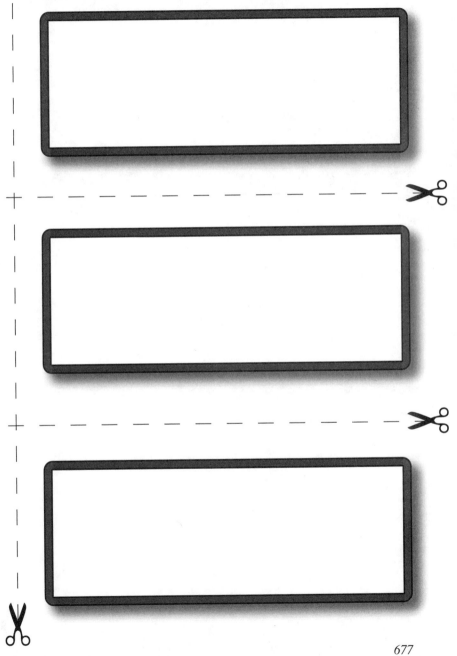

Correct Answers

Index

[Note: Numbers in the Index refer to question numbers.]

[Note: Numbers in the Index refer to question numbers.]

[Note: Numbers in the Index refer to question numbers.]

[Note: Numbers in the Index refer to question numbers.]

[Note: Numbers in the Index refer to question numbers.]

[Note: Numbers in the Index refer to question numbers.]